North Korea's Foreign Relations

Wayne S. Kiyosaki

The Praeger Special Studies program—utilizing the most modern and efficient book production techniques and a selective worldwide distribution network—makes available to the academic, government, and business communities significant, timely research in U.S. and international economic, social, and political development.

North Korea's Foreign Relations

The Politics of Accommodation, 1945-75

PRAEGER SPECIAL STUDIES IN INTERNATIONAL POLITICS AND GOVERNMENT

Praeger Publishers New York Washington London

Library of Congress Cataloging in Publication Data

Kiyosaki, Wayne S
    North Korea's foreign relations.

    (Praeger special studies in international politics and government)
    Bibliography: p.
    Includes index.
    1. Korea (Democratic People's Republic)—Foreign relations. I. Title.
DS935.5.K58   327.519   76-19548
ISBN 0-275-23490-8

PRAEGER PUBLISHERS
111 Fourth Avenue, New York, N.Y. 10003, U.S.A.

Published in the United States of America in 1976
by Praeger Publishers, Inc.

All rights reserved

© 1976 by Wayne S. Kiyosaki

Printed in the United States of America

ACKNOWLEDGMENTS

This book originated as a doctoral dissertation submitted to the Graduate School of Arts and Sciences at George Washington University. I wish to acknowledge the valuable guidance provided by Professor Harold Hinton of George Washington University, under whose direction this study was originally begun. I am also indebted to Dr. Charles Elliott of George Washington University and to Dr. Lyman Miller, a friend and colleague, for their generous comments and suggestions. I am, however, solely responsible for all views expressed in this study. Special thanks also go to Professor Wolfgang Kraus, Professor Kurt London, and Dr. Carl Linden for many years of support and encouragement. Last but not least, I would like to thank my wife Jean, without whose sacrifice this study would have been impossible.

CONTENTS

	Page
ACKNOWLEDGMENTS	v
INTRODUCTION	viii

Chapter

1 THE FOUR-POWER ALIGNMENT IN THE KOREAN PENINSULA ... 1

    The Role of China ... 2
    The Role of the Soviet Union ... 4
    The Role of the United States ... 7
    The Role of Japan ... 9
    The Delicate Balance in Korea ... 11
    Notes ... 13

2 LEADERSHIP AND THE POLITICAL IDEOLOGY OF KIM IL-SONG ... 19

    The Cult of Kim Il-song ... 19
    The Ideological Component ... 21
    The National Component ... 25
    The Nature of the Policy Mechanism ... 27
    Notes ... 31

3 THE IMPACT OF STALIN AND STALINISM: 1945-53 ... 33

    The Initial Stage of Diplomacy ... 33
    Prelude to the Korean War ... 35
    The Korean War and the Aftermath ... 37
    The Initial Limits of Chinese Influence in Pyongyang ... 40
    The Rise of Kim Il-song and the Death of Stalin ... 43
    Notes ... 45

4 RECONSTRUCTION AND THE PROBLEM OF KHRUSHCHEV: 1954-64 ... 48

    The Reconstruction Period ... 49

Chapter	Page
The Impact of the CPSU Twentieth Party Congress	51
The Sino-Soviet Rift: New Dimensions in the National Interest	53
The Management of Pressures from the Chinese	57
The Fall of Khrushchev: The End of an Era	60
Notes	62

5 THE PERILS OF INDEPENDENCE AND BELLIGERENCY: 1965-69 66

The Implications of the Kosygin Visit to Pyongyang	67
The Move Back to the Middle	68
The Sino-Korean Rift	71
The Korean Workers' Party Conference of 1966	77
The Radical Turn and the Unification Issue	79
Notes	84

6 CONTROLLED MODERATION AND DETENTE: 1970-75 87

The Chou En-lai Visit to Pyongyang	88
The Fifth Party Congress: Plans for an Uncertain Future	91
The Impact of the Sino-American Detente	95
North-South Contacts and the Unification Issue	98
The Realities of Coexistence	100
Notes	105

7 CONCLUSION 110

SELECTED BIBLIOGRAPHY 115

INDEX 130

ABOUT THE AUTHOR 135

INTRODUCTION

This book covers the broad outlines of North Korea's foreign relations from 1945 to 1975. The circumstances under which Pyongyang has had to define its relationship to other countries are traced and the manner in which it has responded to the challenges raised under those circumstances is analyzed.

The basic assumption here is that there are two traits underlying North Korea's foreign relations. First, there is North Korea's inordinate sensitivity to external pressures and influences. Second, there is an underlying wariness over the strength of the imperatives of a new Socialist morality that must be assured to achieve internal cohesiveness in the face of such pressures and influences. Both features serve to underscore a feeling that runs deep in Pyongyang that it needs the time and opportunity to set its own house in order without foreign encumbrances.

Since its founding, the Democratic People's Republic of Korea (DPRK) has always been cast in the role of a small country caught between great power interests. The problem has been endemic to Korean history. Even today, American, Russian, Chinese, and Japanese interests still continue to weigh in some form or another on policy options being considered in Pyongyang. The wariness that each of those countries has displayed toward each other as protagonists or as competitors has also been the measure of the wariness displayed by the North Koreans themselves over the shifting motives of those countries. In Pyongyang, the concern is that it has too often been the unwilling pawn of great power conflicts.

Of the four countries, the Soviet Union and China in particular have heavily influenced North Korea since 1945. But Pyongyang's accommodation to pressures from Moscow and Peking has never resulted in passive acquiescence to their demands. In every instance, Pyongyang has resorted to a policy of positive accommodation in its relations with the two countries. For example, in the period immediately following the liberation of Korea in 1945, Kim Il-song used the support of the Soviet military occupation command to destroy his political opposition just as the Soviet command used him to solidify Soviet influence in North Korea. During the Korean War, Kim Il-song also employed the Chinese presence in Pyongyang to wean North Korea away from Soviet dominance. Moreover, when the Sino-Soviet dispute erupted, Kim used the situation to expand Pyongyang's independence at the expense of the two feuding powers.

As a result, it is hardly adequate to analyze the North Korean experience in foreign affairs purely in terms of the totalitarian concept.[1] From a conceptual standpoint, there are developmental and cultural approaches that provide far more promising approaches to the study of North Korea's foreign relations simply because Pyongyang's differences with countries like the Soviet Union and China have arisen as much from cultural differences as they have from ideological differences.[2] Kim Il-song has bent Marxism-Leninism to his liking at every turn of the North Korean path to communism to tailor it to "conditions in North Korea."

The theoretical claims of this book are minimal. Although it has benefited from the theoretical insights of the other scholars, no attempt has been made to adhere rigorously to a systems approach. It should be noted, however, that other Korean scholars have contributed studies embodying some of the more recent conceptual approaches to the study of Communist systems. Ilpyong Kim's study dealing with North Korea's attempts to transform a traditional and backward society into a modern industrial society, embodied Tucker's "cultural" concept and Kautsky's model of communism as a system of forced modernization.[3] On the other hand, Byung Chul Koh's study on North Korea's foreign policy relied on an analytical framework conceived by Jan Triska to study Soviet foreign policy in terms of five component parts.[4]

Whereas Kim's analysis is concerned primarily with North Korea's efforts to gird internally to build a modern society, which he then discusses in terms of its implications for North Korea's foreign relations in his final chapter, this book is weighted more heavily to North Korea's foreign relations with less emphasis on Socialist transformation in the domestic sector. Hopefully, this study will add a foreign relations dimension to Kim's skillful analysis.

On the other hand, this book adds to Koh's study by expanding on his coverage. The effort here is also to give greater currency to the role of the great powers in shaping North Korea's foreign relations and to give greater emphasis to the subjective aspects of North Korea's foreign policy. North Korea's subjectivity, which is implicit in Koh's objective analysis of its foreign relations, deserves to be underscored even more heavily. Pyongyang's subjectivity, which is generically inherent in the meaning of chuche, must be understood not only as a key element in North Korea's attitude toward other countries but also as the basis of its undoing as a militant country given to periods of unpredictability. Herein lies the threat of North Korea as a potential tinderbox that could ignite another incident in the Korean peninsula. North Korea's bellicosity, its unyielding attitude toward outsiders, and the arrogance of its claims provide an image of toughness characteristic of the spartan attitude that is now being cultivated internally. However, at the same time it belies an undercurrent of doubt whether it will ever be successful in its drive for self-strengthening in the face of the predatory incursions of bourgeois capitalists as well as Socialist imperialists. If there has been what can be characterized as a bizarre side to North Korea's international behavior, it can probably be traced to the basic frustrations of a country still faced by what it regards as a hostile environment that forces unwanted outside choices on a country bent on self-reliance and self-determination.

Finally, a word is in order for the contributions of the study on Korean communism by professors Scalapino and Lee, which is a standard work for all students of North Korean politics.[5] The study opened the way for North Korea's political dynamics to be viewed as something other than an offshoot of a political process orchestrated by the great powers. In spite of the enormous intertwining influence of the great powers, it is only in the context of North Korea's perception of the political opportunities offered in the Korean peninsula that one can, for example, develop an appreciation of Pyongyang's concept of chuche. By taking the concept of chuche and systematically assessing the manner in which it has become a factor in the politics of the Korean peninsula, Scalapino and Lee have enjoined students of North Korean politics to look to the dynamics in Pyongyang as another source of insight into the nature of North Korea's relations with other countries. The Scalapino-Lee study has also provided fresh insights into the manner in which the North Korean brand of communism has paralleled and diverged from the brand of communism championed by Moscow and Peking. Like the imperial culturalists of yore, the North Koreans today are convinced that the Koreanization of Russian and Chinese examples has produced a model for communism inferior to none. The Scalapino-Lee study is also unique because it utilizes personal interviews of people who had once lived under the North Korean system to corroborate speculations drawn from Pyongyang's vernacular publications. Although some biases and distortions can be expected from interview techniques, in the case of North Korea, the present state of knowledge makes it imperative to rely on such techniques. Published sources from North Korea tend to raise formidable obstacles for all outside observers of the country.

Among Western observers in particular, there is a common tendency to view the communications from Pyongyang as being overly chauvinistic, rhetorically turgid, and excessively repetitive, especially in praise of Kim Il-song. To many, they are propaganda and not news or information. The view is well founded but it should be noted that much of the so-called propaganda carried in the vernacular press is directed to the masses. It is an instrument of indoctrination attuned to North Korean perceptions and, as such, there is method in what often appears to be madness. The outside observer is hampered by the fact that North Korea is a denied area to all but a handful of Americans, making broadcasts and open publications from Pyongyang almost the only sources of information available on the DPRK.

I am greatly indebted to the pioneering work of other American and Korean scholars on North Korean politics. However, many of the most significant insights gained in conducting this study were derived from reading the open sources from Pyongyang.* Although many of the publications from Pyongyang appear in English, some of the most useful information is to be found in Korean language sources. This is due to the strong domestic focus of the vernacular newspapers and magazines. Within North Korea itself, along with the wall newspapers and bulletins, the daily newspaper serves as the major instrument of communications with the masses in all parts of the country. In a country where the technical, cultural, and ideological revolutions are all being carried out simultaneously, a proper transmission of directives is imperative. While it is highly likely that all Party directives are transmitted through private channels of communications, it is highly unlikely that a mass understanding of the directives can be accomplished without the use of the mass media.[6] For cadres and responsible functionaries, newspaper editorials and commentaries are useful vehicles for the conduct of expository discussions on strategies that link theory and practice, and for the explanation of policies.

In that regard, repetitiveness is an asset to the North Korean media. The steady drumfire of ideological reminders keeps the masses aware of their responsibilities to Pyongyang's action programs. It is part of the program of mass indoctrination that requires a consciousness of purpose at all times.

Moreover, the press provides a barometer of priorities. The prominence given to certain events, to certain state guests or personalities, to basic political-ideological themes, and, of course, to status symbols that accrue to members of the leadership by virtue of their ranking or orders of appearance are all matters that are carefully arranged to provide the proper visual impact on the readership. Moreover, like languages all over the world, there are certain nuances that can only be conveyed in Korean.

---

*The major North Korean publications are the Nodong Sinmun (The Workers' Newspaper), a daily newspaper published by the Korean Workers' Party; the Minju Choson (Democratic Korea), a newspaper representing the governmental organs; the Nodong Ch'ongnyon (Working Youths), an organ of the Youth League; and Kulloja (Worker), the Party theoretical journal.

Foreign and domestic issues also tend to be discussed in the arcane language of the media. Up until the death of Stalin, Pyongyang had helped to preserve a facade of monolithic unity within the bloc. However, once the Sino-Soviet dispute was surfaced and open communications became the basis of ventilating differences between Moscow and Peking, the problem of addressing themselves to the split also became a problem for Pyongyang. The inferences drawn from such discussions can, of course, prove illusory, especially in light of our inaccessibility to private Party discussions or secret documents. There can only be speculation as to how and why certain decisions are reached. However, a systematic examination of Party newspapers, journals, and other publications often offer insights into the manner in which foreign and domestic issues are confronted by the Party elite. The lodes are often in obscure crannies but they are there to be mined.

Finally, there are the ubiquitous quotes from Kim Il-song, which, like most political aphorisms, tend to be far more didactic than informative. But, while it is easy to be lulled into neglect by the banal rhetoric and interminable quotes from "the esteemed and beloved leader," the weight that many of Kim Il-song's statements carry is unquestionable and must be scrutinized with current issues in mind. For example, Kim's "Theses on the Socialist Agrarian Question" of 1964 are still widely quoted with obvious references to current agricultural issues. The weight and relevance of current statements tend to gain added credence when supported by quotations from Kim Il-song.[7]

The basic method of Kremlinology adopted for this book was therefore influenced considerably by the very nature of the North Korean media, the ambiguity of its communications, and Pyongyang's inaccessibility to most Western observers.

Throughout, primary reliance is placed on the McCune-Reischauer system of romanization, except where an alteration of a more commonly known spelling would have proven misleading.

NOTES

1. In the 1960s, scholars such as Alfred G. Meyer began to point to some of the inherent shortcomings of the totalitarian approach employed in Russian studies that tended to overemphasize the dominance of Soviet power in bloc relations. It was also noted with dissatisfaction that political scientists had failed to apply many of the new concepts developed in the comparative study of political systems to area studies. See Alfred G. Meyer, "The Comparative Study of Communist Political Systems," Slavic Review 26 (1967):

3-12. Other works in support of that view include Robert C. Tucker, "Communist Revolutions, National Culture, and Divided Nations," Studies in Comparative Communism 7, no. 3 (Autumn 1974): 235-45; and John H. Kautsky, "Communism and the Comparative Development," Slavic Review 26 (1967): 13-17.

    2. Alex Inkeles describes the "developmental model" as one that "deals with certain problems common to all developing societies," and one that "tries to treat the distinctive problems of a particular society, but always from the perspective of development." He suggests the developmental model as an additional model to the totalitarian model. Alex Inkeles, Social Change in Soviet Russia (Cambridge, Mass.: Harvard University Press, 1968), p. 422. Robert C. Tucker has noted that often disagreements such as those relating to the Sino-Soviet dispute have arisen as much from "a clash of cultures" as they have from power struggles over such "tangible things" as "territory . . . or a historic enmity between Russians and Chinese." Robert C. Tucker, "Culture, Political Culture, and Communist Society," Political Science Quarterly 88, no. 2 (June 1973): 189.

    3. Ilpyong J. Kim, Communist Politics in North Korea (New York: Praeger, 1975).

    4. Under Triska's frame of reference, there are five parts to foreign policy: (1) ideology, (2) strategy, (3) operational direction, (4) tactics, and (5) propaganda. Byung Chul Koh, The Foreign Policy of North Korea (New York: Praeger, 1969), pp. xvii-xviii.

    5. Robert A. Scalapino and Chong-Sik Lee, "The Origins of the Korean Communist Movement," Journal of Asian Studies 20, no. 1 (November 1960): 9-31; 20, no. 2 (February 1961): 149-67.

    6. The purposes and functions of the Party newspaper, the Nodong Sinmun, are discussed in O Ki-wan, "Nodong Sinmun ui Naemak" (An Inside Account of the Nodong Sinmun), Pukhan (North Korea), no. 12 (1974): 266-73.

    7. Aside from the various editions of the collected works of Kim Il-song, one of the most useful references on Kim's thoughts is an index to statements attributed to him. See, Kim Il-song Tongji ui Nojak Saekin (Index to the Works of Kim Il-song), (Pyongyang: The DPRK Academy of Social Sciences Publishing House, 1970).

North Korea's
Foreign Relations

CHAPTER

1

THE FOUR-POWER ALIGNMENT IN THE KOREAN PENINSULA

The revolutionary line of the Democratic People's Republic of Korea (DPRK) is national identity in ideology, independence in politics, self-reliance in economics, and self-defense in national defense. As a statement of purpose, its affirmations are positive. In reality, as a positive expression of political certitude, its affirmations have been as much a product of despair as they have been of hope. The reasons are embedded in the geopolitical history of Korea and its tradition of accommodation with great power politics.

For centuries, Korea was forced to shape a national life under Chinese suzerainty and when Chinese influence began to wane, it provided the setting for Sino-Japanese and Russo-Japanese conflicts of interest.[1] In 1910, Korea was annexed by Japan as a colony. The promises of independence and self-determination did not again emerge until World War II began to draw to a close. Yet, soon after liberation, Korean hopes were again quickly thwarted as American-Soviet differences quickly turned Korea into opposing North-South camps divided at the thirty-eighth parallel.

In June 1950, with apparent Sino-Soviet blessings, the militant North Korean regime, headed by Kim Il-song, attempted to forcibly unify Korea. The war failed to achieve the most coveted goal of national unification. It also left Pyongyang in shambles, the casualty rate was high, large-scale defections to the South eroded its relatively low population base, and it established a reputation for militancy in the North that continues to make it a possible flash point for future international military confrontations. It also marked China's return to the international scene as a major contender for great power recognition with obvious implications for future intrabloc relations. What was evident in Pyongyang as early as 1945 was amply confirmed by the late 1950s--that the Chinese and the Russians were opposing contenders for power and influence within the bloc and it meant that any future plans for Korean reunification would be without the former presumption of Sino-Soviet solidarity.[2]

The Sino-Soviet dispute forced an altered approach to foreign relations in Pyongyang. The clash between the two neighboring giants raised new threats to Pyongyang as its leaders faced the perilous prospect of treading a neutral course between Moscow and Peking.*

The DPRK's attempts to find its own way demonstrated Pyongyang's limited purchase over the very conditions that forced an independent course on it. However, the cult of Kim Il-song that emerged under those circumstances demonstrated the Pyongyang media's mettle for historical and ideological exegesis. Today, according to the North Korean media, it is the DPRK, led by Kim Il-song and not the Soviet Union or China, that is to be credited with "defeating" Japan during World War II. Repeated incantations among the masses about such "great achievements" now give proper public form to the ritual of "standing up" to outside aggression, and it has also provided a useful mechanism for internal mobilization against external pressures.

THE ROLE OF CHINA

Chinese influence in Korea has been aided by China's size and proximity. China's size gave it dominance, and proximity afforded it cultural influence. Of all the neighboring countries, China cast the dominant influence on Korea. Historically, a strong and vibrant China, favorably disposed toward Korea, assured peace and stability. Conversely, as a tributary state under Chinese suzerainty, a troubled or vindictive China was capable of spelling trouble for Korea. Yet, for centuries, the relationship was loose enough to allow Korea to opt for a policy of isolationism.

While Korea was greatly influenced by Chinese culture, much of the process was accomplished through an integration of Chinese elements into Korean culture, and the belief persisted among the Koreans that they had created a distinct culture of their own that was inferior to none. In that regard, however, the sense of unity that emerged in the country was keyed to culture and a racially homogeneous citizenry, and not politically to a centralized Korean government.[3] As a result, the lack of widespread public identity with a

---

*Pyongyang shares a boundary in excess of 1,400 miles with the PRC and a lesser border of slightly over 10 miles with the USSR. However, the distance between the Soviet-Korean border and Vladivostok is only about 78 miles.

central political authority at the national level hampered Korea's quest for nationalism.[4]

In both China and Korea, nationalism emerged out of a condition of national humiliation imposed by outside powers. Both sides also suffered from internal bickering and factionalism in the face of those external challenges.[5] The revolutionary struggles on both sides have therefore been directed most forcefully at elements of the old culture that continue to stand in the way of the new revolutionary transformations.

China's impact on Korea came by way of its domination of the Asian continent in the past. For the lesser countries of Asia, survival was often dependent upon choosing between contending powers and going with the stronger of the powers. In Korea, that approach to international relations has come to be regarded as sadaejuui, or "flunkeyism."[6]

China, having been the dominant outside power in Korea for so long and having suffered virtually the same fate as Korea at the hands of the great powers, has at least been in a position to understand the Korean distrust of outsiders and also the untoward reaction that an overbearing attitude could trigger in Pyongyang. In that respect, a shared reliance on the Sinitic culture has contributed to a close understanding of objectives on both sides.

Nevertheless, the North Koreans have complained that the Chinese, along with the Russians, have practiced "great power chauvinism" on occasion, at the expense of the North Koreans.[7] The North Koreans found the attitude of Moscow and Peking to be particularly abrasive as both sides attempted to draw other parties to their own side during the initial stages of the Sino-Soviet dispute.

Inasmuch as Peking holds one of the major keys to the DPRK's security, North Korea has been quite circumspect in its criticism of PRC domestic policy. However, this has not deterred Pyongyang from criticizing Peking whenever Chinese policy has appeared to detract from North Korean or bloc interests. This was particularly true during the Chinese Cultural Revolution when the North Koreans indicated that the Chinese were remiss in mobilizing and unleashing the Red Guards for political purposes under the pretense of waging a cultural revolution.[8] In spite of the extraordinary emphasis placed by the Koreans themselves on the cult of Kim Il-song, Pyongyang also showed signs of displeasure over the presence of a revolutionary committee standing above the Chinese Party structure.[9] Such alleged indiscretions and Chinese adventurism allowed the North Koreans to reject Chinese advice and effectively seal off the DPRK from any influence stemming from the Chinese Cultural Revolution.*

---

*The North Korean press shunned ever mentioning or discussing the Chinese Cultural Revolution or the domestic political upheavals

The Red Guards retaliated by posting insulting remarks about Kim Il-song on their wall posters. The ill feeling between Pyongyang and Peking did not abate until the Ninth Congress of the Chinese Communist Party signaled an end to the radical phase of the Cultural Revolution. By then, the Brezhnev Doctrine had increased the possibility of a Soviet invasion of China and the Nixon Doctrine had threatened to leave a power vacuum in the Asia-Pacific region for Moscow to exploit, which left Peking with no alternative but to move to stabilize the situation in the Korean Peninsula.

To face its common "enemies," the United States and the USSR, Peking's strategy was to muster support, and it was to its advantage to have Pyongyang in tow since North Korea's virulent hatred of the United States was balanced by an obvious disinclination by Kim Il-song to disagree too violently with Moscow. Neither Pyongyang nor Moscow could afford to and Peking knew it. Pyongyang's support, therefore, fit in well with Peking's plan to treat the United States and the USSR as separate categories of enemies. To this day, Peking has been careful not to antagonize these "enemies" to the point where both would feel compelled to unite against China. Meanwhile, in return for its support, Peking has provided Pyongyang with access to the Third World, where its reliance on the superpowers would not have to be as pronounced, and where more sympathetic support could be expected for Korean unification.[10]

THE ROLE OF THE SOVIET UNION

In 1945, Soviet control over North Korean affairs was based on the control of the personnel and the political apparatus established under the auspices of the Soviet occupation command in Pyongyang. The level of Soviet influence was also aided considerably by Kim Il-song's special relationship with Stalin. It was Stalin who placed Kim in power. Kim's allegiance to Stalin, which was reinforced by a strong Asian belief in personal obligation and loyalty, allowed Stalin's influence to be carried right into Pyongyang's inner policymaking councils. Once Stalin passed away, however, the accessibility that was an inherent part of the Stalin-Kim relationship died with him.

---

associated with it. The North Korean media has always avoided open discussions about the internal affairs of others, but in the case of the Cultural Revolution, it was probably done to prevent the spread of the revolutionary Chinese mania into Pyongyang. Pyongyang also took advantage of the lull in diplomacy with Peking to purge all leaders suspected of pro-Chinese leanings. Included among them were Political Committee members Kim Ch'ang-man and Kim Kwang-hyop.

It meant that the personal accessibility that the Kremlin once enjoyed was closed off and accessibility had to be gained through normal bureaucratic channels. Khrushchev's influence in Pyongyang would probably have been much greater had he taken the trouble to open his own private channel of communications with Kim Il-song. However, Khrushchev's denigration of Stalin, which triggered an attack by North Korean Party Central Committee dissidents on Kim himself, all but foreclosed that possibility. At that point, the North Koreans were in complete control of the political-bureaucratic apparatus and it ushered in a growing sense of autonomy in Pyongyang.[11]

The decline of Soviet influence during the Khrushchev era was also influenced by the circumstances that forced the North Koreans to make a choice between Soviet-style or Chinese-style socialism during the early stages of the Sino-Soviet dispute. Pyongyang's choice was a Korean-style socialism. But, the choice of a Korean-style socialism was motivated by Asiatic conditions and in spite of vehement assertions of its independence and originality, the specifically Asian requirements placed it closer in both practice and theory to the Chinese-style of socialism. Therefore, any disagreement that Moscow was to have had with Peking on the ideological issues underlying their separate approaches to socialism was bound to have a fallout effect on the North Koreans.

Like China, North Korea embarked on a program of industrialization against Soviet advice. The severe ordeals that resulted from their attempt to carry out an accelerated program of agricultural collectivization while preparing for industrialization was also aggravated by developments stemming from the Communist Party of the Soviet Union's (CPSU) Twentieth Party Congress. Khrushchev's formulations on liberalization and de-Stalinization, on the possibility of relying on peaceful means to achieve a proletarian revolution, and on peaceful coexistence were all eventually discredited in Pyongyang.[12] The anticult revolt against Kim, the riots in Hungary, the dissident rallies in Poland, and the instabilities surfaced by the Hundred Flowers movement in China all tended to reinforce Kim's distrust of Khrushchev.

Moreover, Pyongyang's opposition was also registered against Moscow's heralding of a "state of the whole people," representing "a total and final victory for socialism." Pyongyang's position was that such a view would lead to an abandonment of the "class struggle" and a surrender to "counterrevolutionary economism," a condition that would be intolerable in North Korea.[13] Such differences over basic political-ideological issues laid the groundwork for Soviet-Korean differences that were later carried over to other international differences.

As soon as it became evident that Moscow would not be able to influence Pyongyang at will, a switch to dominance became evident in the Kremlin. Soviet-American detente, the conclusion of a Soviet-West German Treaty--which dealt a blow against the DPRK formula for Korean unification--the improvement of Soviet-Japanese relations, and informal Soviet contacts with Taiwan and South Korea, all caused aggravations in Pyongyang. To add insult to injury, Moscow openly downgraded the role and thoughts of Kim Il-song.[14]

Moscow's main concern in the 1970s continues to be the containment of China. The problem of Korea persists as part of that concern. Moscow remains aware that a reoccurrence of the kind of adventurism that marked North Korea's behavior in 1968 and 1969 could involve the Soviet Union in a nuclear exchange with the United States under the terms of the DPRK-USSR security pact of 1961.[15] Although Moscow initially showed signs of being wary of Peking's instigation of North Korean adventurism, the U.S.-PRC rapprochement and the undiminished buildup of Soviet forces along the Chinese border have since tended to lessen the Kremlin's concern about that possibility.*

Thus, although Pyongyang has leaned more toward Peking than Moscow since 1970, the arrangement has been acceptable since a major part of Peking's burden in keeping North Korea in tow has been to put a damper on North Korea's militancy while sponsoring Pyongyang's phased entry into a wider international order. This has freed Moscow of that burden. Meanwhile, Pyongyang's snub of Moscow allows the Kremlin to provide only perfunctory support for the DPRK's stand on unification. It has been easier on Moscow to trumpet loud calls for an American withdrawal from South Korea. Calls for a forcible removal of the United States, besides being unrealistic, could only complicate Moscow's concern for detente.[16] At the same time, Moscow is aware that Kim Il-song's intense concern for Korean "independence" will never allow him to sever his ties with the Soviet Union.† In that respect, and despite its open discord with Peking, perhaps there is one point on which the Kremlin can agree with Mao: "One can drink water from the same river, but it is difficult to straddle two boats; giving the appearance of accord but divided in heart is easier said than done."

---

*The visit of Soviet Marshal Zakharov to Pyongyang right after Chou En-lai's departure seems to indicate that the Kremlin was concerned about possible North Korean moves to instigate the Chinese.

†The North Koreans apparently balked at the inclusion of a hegemony clause in the DPRK-PRC joint communique of April 1975, which was probably appreciated in the Kremlin.

FOUR-POWER ALIGNMENT

THE ROLE OF THE UNITED STATES

Anti-imperialist attitudes appear particularly harsh in Pyongyang. The most obvious target of that attitude is the United States. Yet, the U.S. involvement in the affairs of the DPRK was due more to circumstance than to design. Historically, there had been no close ties between the United States and Korea, a factor that was contributed to by Korea's geographical remoteness, and there was no commercial or economic interest to lure the United States into a kind of involvement that might conceivably have been regarded as "colonialist" or "imperialist."[17]

The American concern for Korea's future was echoed in the Cairo Declaration of December 1, 1943, in which the United States, China, and Britain declared that, "mindful of the enslavement of the people of Korea," the three powers are "determined that in due course Korea shall become free and independent."[18] Out of that initial declaration, there evolved an agreement between the United States, Britain, and the Soviet Union in June 1945 to establish a four-power trusteeship for Korea.

However, soon after the end of World War II, the world began to polarize around the United States and the USSR, leaving the fate of Korea to the international system that had evolved under that bipolar alignment.[19] The arrangements, which called for the division of Korea at the thirty-eighth parallel to allow Soviet forces to accept the surrender of Japanese forces in the North and the United States in the South, soon became permanently frozen as Cold War differences mounted between the United States and the Soviet Union.

In June 1950, when North Korean forces launched a surprise attack on the South to remedy the divisiveness wrought on the Koreans by great power disagreements, it was a UN intervention, spearheaded by U.S. forces, that prevented a Northern takeover of the South. Immediately, the South, from which U.S. forces had previously been withdrawn, became identified with the interests of the United States. The alarm in Washington was not over North Korea but over the Soviet Union. The North Korean invasion was interpreted as a new turn in Soviet foreign policy.

> The Korean war was interpreted by Acheson and most others in the State Department, as well as the Joint Chiefs of Staff, as ushering in a new phase of Soviet foreign policy. Their view, which Truman accepted, was that having launched an attack on Korea--the first case of Communist open use of naked military force to expand the

system--the Soviet Union was likely to call on
satellite armies elsewhere, particularly in East
Germany, to spread Communist control.[20]

From the American standpoint, the North Korean attack could hardly have been launched without some form of Soviet aid and encouragement.[21] Because of that, the U.S. presence in South Korea soon became a part of the U.S. policy of Soviet containment. American military aid soon followed to build up the defense potential in the South to make it an active part of the overall strategy to oppose communism in the Far East.

The buildup of the Republic of Korea (ROK) also coincided with U.S. efforts to bolster Japan in the face of the rising threat of China. In other words, the North Korean invasion forced the United States to place an even greater stake in the security of both South Korea and Japan. Since then, the U.S. military presence in South Korea and the key role that it has played in the rapid progress of both the ROK and Japan has made the United States the target of much propaganda abuse as the greatest obstacle to the reunification of Korea in Pyongyang.

The U.S. involvement in Vietnam in the 1960s only reinforced North Korean suspicions about American motives. A rising level of prosperity coupled with the introduction of bourgeois culture into Seoul was seen as a wider struggle to undermine the South internally to perpetuate the division and, ultimately, a base of reaction to undermine the North.[22] North Korea's main objection to the Sino-Soviet dispute in the 1960s revolved around the belief that the U.S. strategy was to concentrate on the small countries and dispose of them one by one while Moscow and Peking quarreled. At the height of its frustration, Pyongyang turned to the tactics of dramatization. In 1968, Pyongyang captured the USS Pueblo and in 1969, shot down an American EC-121. The first incident exposed America's vulnerability. The second did not. The United States could easily have devastated Pyongyang. The alarmed leadership in Moscow moved quickly to cool the situation. The Soviet reaction confirmed the suspicion of Pyongyang that Moscow cannot be relied on in any serious confrontation with the United States, and in Moscow it quickly became evident that Pyongyang's excessive zealousness had to be curbed. Ironically, Pyongyang reinforced Moscow's conviction of the correctness of detente, to which North Korea was unalterably opposed.

In the 1970s, Pyongyang's switch to the Chinese line has not lessened its level of accommodation with the U.S. presence in spite of the U.S. withdrawal from Vietnam. The American-Chinese rapprochement has, in fact, forced changes in Pyongyang's approach to its foreign policy. The suspension of confrontations now makes it imperative for Pyongyang to seek gains through more conventional channels of diplomacy. Moreover, it is aware that as long as the Sino-Soviet dispute persists against the background of a possible intrabloc confrontation, there will be little inclination on the part of either Moscow or Peking to have the United States withdraw precipitously from Korea. As long as that condition prevails, the U.S. role in Korea will continue to be primarily a problem of the great powers and secondarily, a problem of the DPRK. Yet, all of the major powers are aware that Pyongyang is capable of embarking on a rash course that could upset the delicate balance of detente.

THE ROLE OF JAPAN

Japan's rise to great power status was marked by military victories in the Sino-Japanese War of 1895 and the Russo-Japanese War of 1905. The two incidents led to the effective removal of Soviet and Chinese influence from Korea and the ultimate annexation of Korea on August 22, 1910 as a colony of Japan.

Pyongyang has emphasized that foreign intrusions during that era hindered progress in Korea because "the feudal Yi Dynasty obediantly opened the door to the invasion of the capitalist powers in order to maintain their feudal rule."[23] The Japanese role was regarded to have been the introduction of "finance capital" into Korea and the willful imposition of a colonialist system on the country, which made the Korean economy an extension of the Japanese economy rather than a self-sustaining Korean economy.

The residual effects of that Japanese experience seem to appear in different forms in Pyongyang. The most obvious manifestation is a harshly anti-Japanese attitude. It provides a bitter focal point of discontent, which is kept alive by the propaganda media for political and ideological reasons.* For purposes of official historiography, the era signifies the beginning of what is commonly referred to as "the glorious revolutionary tradition of anti-Japanese struggle organized directly by the great revolutionary leader, Comrade Kim Il-song." The emphasis is on the positive side of the "struggle," as opposed to Korea's long-standing vulnerability to foreign aggression. More significantly, it marks the revolutionary "coming" of Kim Il-song. It is also the period in which the Leninist theory of imperialism is linked to the Korean experience. This has allowed Kim Il-song to be depicted as the lone figure divined by fate to lead all

---

*Pyongyang is careful to point out that the enmity is not directed toward the Japanese people, but toward "reactionary" leadership.

Koreans out of imperialist bondage and it has legitimized his attempts to infuse North Korean political and ideological campaigns with large doses of Leninism, a key feature of which is the use of authoritative Leninist prescriptions to consolidate domestic unity under the "dictatorship of the proletariat."[24]

The Sino-Soviet dispute made North Korea's accentuation of its own revolutionary tradition both politically opportune and comforting. It allowed the North Koreans to credit themselves for their own revolutionary tradition by going back to the anti-Japanese partisan era. This has been coupled with discreet efforts to avoid mentioning the signal contributions made by the Russians, Chinese, and the Americans during the same period. Although the Russian and Chinese contributions are appreciated and lauded, they tend to be treated as separate subjects and are not allowed to detract from the laudatory accounts of Korean contributions to the Korean revolution against the Japanese.

There is also a discernible resentment against Japan's membership in a Western and virtually all-white circle of rich nations.[25] In addition, there is an underlying suspicion echoed by the broadcast and press media that beneath the veneer of economic affluence lurks Japan's hopes for a revival of Japanese militarism and a modern variant of a Greater East Asia Co-Prosperity Sphere.

On the other hand, there is a more positive side to the DPRK attitude toward Japan. It is rooted in the realization that there is a potential for beneficial economic, scientific, and technical relations with Japan as well as with other capitalistic nations of the world that offer a far more flexible alternative to economic development programs that rely solely on Moscow and Peking.[26] Over the years, the Kremlin has been noted for driving hard terms of agreement on aid, trade, and payments. On the other hand, in contrast to the accelerated economic growth in Japan, China's program of self-reliance, which North Korea has also embraced out of a wariness of outside intrusion, has tended to produce orderly but undramatic rates of growth not entirely in keeping with growing North Korean aspirations.[27]

For very practical reasons, therefore, North Korea's attitude toward Japan has shifted with fundamental changes in the international order. After World War II, a defeated and economically weak Japan was a target of scorn but even that scorn was tempered by a sense of foreboding. Prior to Japan's postwar revival, Kim Il-song was quoted as saying that, "we regard any nation that conspires to revive Japan as an imperialist nation as an enemy of our people."[28]

Ironically, it was the Korean War that contributed directly to Japan's reemergence as a major Asian economic power.[29] The Korean War also contributed to making Japan the cornerstone of the

U.S. anti-Communist strategy in the Far East. Japan's mutual security pact and economic and political ties with the United States, its proximity, which made it the closest nation of the capitalistic camp to the DPRK, and its increasing ties with South Korea made Japan appear to be a growing threat to North Korea and to its plans for unification.[30]

A key step in the direction of increased political involvement in Japan occurred when the Korean Workers' Party (KWP) wrested control over the General Federation of Koreans Residing in Japan from the Japanese Communist Party in 1955. That development was soon followed by the appointment of Pak Song-ch'ol as the Foreign Minister of the DPRK in October 1958, in place of the Soviet-trained Nam Il.[31] Control over the Federation in Japan provided the DPRK with a well-established conduit for political activities and a promising lead into centers of Japanese trade, industry, and technology.

DPRK initiatives in Japan were greatly influenced by the shifting conditions of the 1960s. The most significant development was the rising power of Japan in the face of a declining American presence in 1969. Unlike China and North Korea, the Japanese approach toward self-reliance was to "strengthen and improve" rather than to abandon the existing world economic order. The contrast in results was startling. The Cultural Revolution harmed economic growth in China while military adventurism forced the North Koreans to extend their Seven-Year Plan by three years at a time when the Japanese economy was booming.[32] The response to the Japanese challenge was obvious in Peking and a momentous stage was reached in 1972 when Japanese Premier Kakuei Tanaka journeyed to Peking. In the words of an American observer in Peking at that time, it led to a "de-emphasis of the specter of an aggressive militaristic Japan and a stress on the possibilities of peaceful collaboration."[33] As undesirable as the development might have been for Pyongyang, it had no choice but to go along with Peking. The implications of Sino-Japanese cooperation, especially in light of Peking's determination to become the major outside influence, dictated another accommodation in Pyongyang.

THE DELICATE BALANCE IN KOREA

In the age of detente, the problem of Korea is still tied very closely to the problems of the great powers. The PRC, publicly the most vocal and active supporter of the DPRK, remains committed to the maintenance of stability in the Korean peninsula. It realizes that a sudden move to communize Korea would immediately renew fears of a "dagger pointed at Japan's heart." At the present stage, Peking would prefer an unarmed Japan incapable of military initiatives abroad to an aroused and armed Japan capable of marching on old battlegrounds. As long as Soviet troops are poised along Chinese borders, Peking would prefer anti-Soviet suspicions to anti-Pyongyang suspicions in Tokyo.

On the other hand, the Soviet Union, which is content to let Peking shoulder most of the burden of carrying the DPRK for now, would allow such a burden to have a braking effect on China only to the extent that it does not threaten Moscow's own policy of detente with the United States. It would also be opposed to any military incident on the Korean peninsula that could involve it in a nuclear exchange with the United States, especially with the added possibility of some sort of reprisal from the Chinese. Meanwhile, Moscow will find it to its advantage to use the northern territories issue as a bargaining chip with the Japanese, realizing at the same time that its accessibility to Tokyo must be maintained as long as the Peking-Pyongyang accommodation keeps Moscow at bay in the Far East.

The U.S. presence in South Korea is still the main deterrent to a Northern military offensive against the South. From Peking's viewpoint, the U.S. presence provides a balance against a menacing Soviet presence and the need for a more positive Japanese military role in South Korea. Although Kim Il-song made considerable propaganda mileage by accusing the United States of using the "UN signboard" to justify its presence in South Korea, the elimination of the UN Command in 1976 will eliminate the issue. Meanwhile, the United States will be free to stay in Korea under a bilateral agreement with Seoul. As long as such an agreement remains in effect, the United States can reject any offer of a DPRK-U.S. treaty to replace the 1953 armistice agreement that would exclude the ROK.

Finally, after 30 years, the Korean Workers' Party still finds ideological remnants of the past deeply embedded in the minds of its own people. To expect the people of the South, in spite of their own problems with autocratic rule, to fall willingly under the spell of Kim, The Sun of the Nation, seems difficult even to contemplate.

The situation is fraught with frustration for Kim Il-song, which is one of the reasons why North Korea still continues to provide a threat to stability in the Korean peninsula. Kim has already demonstrated his willingness to provoke incidents on his own under duress. It may well be that the main threat to detente in the Korean peninsula will not be the big powers but the small powers, who may eventually conclude that there is nothing to be lost by breaking a power balance that excludes small-power interests.

In Pyongyang, there is substance to the fear and suspicion of external powers. It is for that reason that Pyongyang is rushing to mobilize the masses in a "continuing revolution" to destroy all vestiges of the old order that have allowed foreign interests to tamper with Korea's internal affairs and to build a new socialist order capable of shaping its own destinies through its own efforts and resources. For that, Korea's dynastic past, which provides memories of chronically inept court representatives being turned into playthings of the great powers, has amply justified the sacrifices demanded of the masses to implement the visionary schemes of Kim Il-song for national redemption. The cult of Kim Il-song in North Korea has emerged to prevent a reversion to the helplessness of the past. In the ignominy suffered at the hands of "imperialist aggressors," Kim has found a latent and emotionally unifying issue with which to mobilize the people of the DPRK in a Marxist-Leninist orchestrated drive toward national self-strengthening, dignity, and international recognition. The methods, directions, and goals are derivatives of Marxism-Leninism but the catalytic agent is a newly tapped fount of Korean nationalism that North Koreans refer to as Socialist patriotism.

The fall of the Yi Dynasty and the Japanese colonization of Korea that followed in the wake of the dynastic decline is perceived by Pyongyang to be due not only to moral and martial torpor. The national incohesiveness and the ineptitude that emerged from that torpor are considered to be as much a product of effete government and leadership. The cult of Kim Il-song, which has sought to dispel all such reminders of an insecure past, has emerged in the belief that the country has longed to be drawn to the rectitude of a patriot who holds out the promise of a better future for Korea.

NOTES

1. In 1637, angered by Korea's pro-Ming, anti-Manchu attitude, Ch'ing Emperor T'ai-tsung led an army of 100,000 troops into Seoul and captured the Korean king. In 1638, Korea agreed to observe suzerain-vassal relations with the Manchus. Takashi Hatada, A History of Korea, trans. and ed. by Warren W. Smith and Benjamin H. Hazard (Santa Barbara: Clio Press, 1969), p. 80. The Manchu sensitivity to the threat posed by a Korea allied with the Ming is also discussed in Woo-keun Han, The History of Korea (Seoul: Eul-Yoo Publishing Co., 1970), pp. 275-78.

2. Kim Ch'ang-sun, Fifteen-Year History of North Korea, U.S. Joint Publications Research Service, JPRS: 18,925 (April 26, 1963): pp. 31-34. The Korean contingent from Yenan was purposely delayed at the border prior to being allowed entry and then disarmed upon entry into Korea.

3. According to one account, "Despite non-official Confucianist leadership in the struggle for national independence against Japanese rule, both the Confucian ideology and the Confucianists in Korea failed

to give the nation a unified concept for national unity and modernization due to strong Confucian familism in Korea and the Korean Confucian leaders' sadaejuui mentality." Thomas Hosuck Kang, "The Role of Confucian Leadership and Ideology in the Political Development of Korea, 1864-1910," Korean Affairs 3, no. 1 (April 1973): 27.

4. The most comprehensive treatment of nationalism in Korea is contained in Chong-Sik Lee, The Politics of Korean Nationalism (Berkeley: University of California Press, 1963).

5. North Korea has maintained that, "what is fundamental are internal factors. Important as outside support is, it plays only a subsidiary role." Nodong Sinmun, August 12, 1966.

6. Flunkeyism has been described as having "deep historical roots" in North Korea because, "The successive feudal rulers of the country served and worshipped the great powers. They fawned upon and cringed before the great powers and tried to hold on to their reins with the latter's support. . . . This contaminated some people in our country with flunkeyism towards the great powers." Nodong Sinmun, August 12, 1966.

7. The Nodong Sinmun once editorialized that, "the international Communist movement in recent years has been a witness to the fact that the intolerable instances of imposing one's wrong lines and views on other fraternal parties, putting pressure upon those who refuse to accept them, and interfering in others' internal affairs have not yet been eliminated." Nodong Sinmun, August 12, 1966.

8. The North Koreans tended to regard a cultural revolution as a necessary part of socialist and communist construction and, by implication, not a weapon of political struggle. A cultural revolution was considered a means of enhancing education, technology, and ideology. Pak To-su, "Sahoejuui Munhwa Konsol un Chugwon ul Chabun Nodong Kyegup ui Chungyo Immu" (The Important Duty of the Working Class Which Gains Supremacy is to Build a Socialist Culture), Nodong Sinmun, December 15, 1966.

9. In criticizing the "left opportunism of Trotskyites," Pyongyang obliquely reminded Peking that "Trotsky always set himself up as existing above all factions and meddled in non-factionalism. Nevertheless, his actual activities were for the sake of mustering all kinds of factional groups to oppose the Bolshevik Party and its center, Lenin." No Tae-hun, "T'urocchukkijuui" (Trotskyism), Nodong Sinmun, September 15, 1966.

10. In a speech delivered at a North Korean mass meeting, Chang Ch'un-ch'iao stated that, "Being a developing socialist country, China belongs to the Third World" and added that China "will never become a super-power and never seek hegemonism." Nodong Sinmun, September 24, 1975.

11. The manner of change in venue from the personal influence of Stalin and the coercion applied during Khrushchev's time is reflected in Kim Il-song's statement that, "The anti-Party revisionist elements within the Party came out to attack the Party, taking advantage of the complicated situation and banking on the support of outside forces. The anti-Party elements within the Party and their supporters abroad, revisionists--big-power chauvinists, lined up as one in opposition to our Party and resorted to subversive activities in an attempt to overthrow the leadership of our Party and Government." Kim Il-song, <u>Selected Works</u>, vol. 2 (Pyongyang: Foreign Languages Publishing House, 1965), pp. 515-16.

12. Pyongyang's initial response to Khrushchev and the CPSU Twentieth Party Congress was positive. In his report to the Third Party Congress of the KWP, Kim Il-song stated that, "The historic Twentieth Congress of the Communist Party of the Soviet Union adopted a majestic program of struggle . . . to lead the Soviet people towards a new, world historic victory of communism, made a deep-going Marxist-Leninist analysis of a number of questions of principles on the developments in the present international situation and drew conclusions of great practical significance. This gives a strong impetus to the future struggle of the Communist and Workers' Parties of various countries and encourages the people all over the world to a more active struggle for peace, happiness and a big future." <u>Third Congress of the Workers' Party of Korea: Documents and Materials</u> (Pyongyang: Foreign Language Publishing House, 1956), p. 7.

13. The North Koreans have tended to go along with the Chinese view on the need to adhere to the dictatorship of the proletariat even beyond the transitional period. However, at the same time, the North Koreans have criticized the Chinese for "failing to understand the dialectic development of the form and content of the class struggle" and for confusing "the class struggle under the socialist system with the class struggle in the stage of the socialist revolution," with the result that the "working masses" were pitted against each other, "greatly damaging the political and ideological unity of the working masses, which should be the basis of social relations under socialism." Byong-Sik Kim, <u>Modern Korea</u> (New York: International Publishers, 1970), pp. 89-91.

14. For example, in observance of the twenty-fifth anniversary of the founding of the DPRK, a Russian publication noted that, "In battles against the aggressors, the Korean people and their military men, under the leadership of the Korean Workers' Party, have demonstrated high moral and combat qualities, unwavering persistence, and devotion to the cause of freedom, democracy, and socialism. The source of the mass heroism of the Korean patriots was the free

and just nature of the war. The troops were well aware of the fact that they were spilling their blood in the name of the noble goal--defense of freedom and independence of the homeland." There was no mention of Kim Il-song. "On Guard of Socialist Accomplishments," Moscow, Kommunist Vooruzhennykh Sil, no. 20 (October 1973), trans. in Joint Publications Research Service, Translations on North Korea, JPRS 60640 (November 27, 1973): p. 3.

15. During Podgorny's visit to Pyongyang in May 1969, he was careful not to endorse Pyongyang's seizure of the USS Pueblo and the shooting down of the EC-121. The joint communique stated that, "Both sides consider that the espionage activities of U.S. warships and planes near the territories of Korea and the Soviet Union are dangerous acts against the peace and security of the peoples and must be stopped." Pyongyang Times, May 19, 1969.

16. A Soviet source notes that, "In our time it is absurd to consider settlement of the Korean problem by military means. The problem of unification of Korea can be settled only by peaceful means in accordance with the good will of the Korean people themselves." Yu. I. Ognev, "Path to Reunification of Korea and Its Enemies," Moscow, Problemy Dal'nego Vostoka, no. 2 (1972), trans. in Joint Publications Research Service, Problems of the Far East, no. 2 (1972), JPRS 56781 (August 15, 1972): p. 98.

17. Even an adverse critic of U.S. policy in Korea notes that the U.S. landing in Korea in 1945 was "not a reassertion of old imperial interests, as was the case of England, France, and Holland in Southeast Asia," but "a harbinger of America's new role in postwar Asia." Frank Baldwin, ed., Without Parallel (New York: Pantheon Books, 1974), p. 6.

18. U.S. Department of State, A Historical Summary of United States-Korean Relations (Washington, D.C.: U.S. Government Printing Office, November 1962), p. 58.

19. The impact of the "international system" has been regarded as the cause of the "divided status" of countries like Korea and this was "less the result of policies than the consequence of world power relations at the end of the Second World War." John H. Herz, "Korea and Germany as Divided Nations: The Systematic Impact," Asian Survey 15, no. 11 (November 1975): 958.

20. Charles E. Bohlen, Witness to History 1929-1969 (New York: W. W. Norton, 1973), p. 292. The view is also supported in Charles Yost, The Conduct and Misconduct of Foreign Affairs (New York: Random House, 1972), p. 12.

21. Bohlen, op. cit., p. 293.

22. The North Korean media has often complained that "U.S. imperialists" and ROK "splittists," as well as foreign "left and right opportunists" have had a bad influence on "opportunists" at home. In

referring to an earlier incident, Kim Il-song stated that the conspiracy based on revisionism between 1956 and 1957, "coincided with the unprecedented reactionary offensive of the U.S. imperialists and their minions against North Korea." Kim Il-song, Selected Works, op. cit., vol. 2, p. 580.

23. Democratic People's Republic of Korea (Pyongyang: Foreign Languages Publishing House, 1958), p. 52.

24. Kim is credited with ushering "a new era of great national prosperity and gain in strength [for the] first time in 5,000 years [in a land that] had once lost its light." Kulloja, no. 4 (April 1975): 41.

25. Unlike China and Korea, both of which belonged to a kind of Confucian family of nations, Japan quickly adapted to Western legal norms, concepts, and ideas in its international relations. Thus, the Japanese were not only looked upon as "inferior" but as "traitors to the Confucian family of nations." See Paul Hibbert Clyde, The Far East (New York: Prentice-Hall Inc., 1952), p. 256. For a more extensive treatment of the nature of the Chinese world order, see John K. Fairbank, ed., The Chinese World Order: Traditional China's Foreign Relations (Cambridge, Mass.: Harvard University Press, 1968), pp. 257-75, as well as M. Frederick Nelson, Korea and the Old Orders in East Asia (Baton Rouge: Louisiana State University Press, 1946), and Immanuel C. Y. Hsu, China's Entrance Into the Family of Nations: The Diplomatic Phase, 1858-1880 (Cambridge, Mass.: Harvard University Press, 1960).

26. At a meeting of industrial activists, Kim Il-song stated that, "Under the circumstances when the economy is developing rapidly and new economic branches are being created, we cannot satisfactorily meet all our needs if we depend only on socialist markets. Therefore . . . we must actively go out to capitalist markets to purchase materials and machinery that we need." Nodong Sinmun, March 5, 1975. From 1970 to 1973, North Korea's total trade with Japan increased from $57.7 million to $172.4 million. Kankoku-Hoku Chosen Yoran (A Survey of South and North Korea), Sekai Seikei Chosakaihen (Compilations of the Research Association for the World Political Economies) (Tokyo, 1974), p. 303.

27. Pyongyang has had to be wary of economic growth in the South. In 1960, prior to the Pak takeover, the growth rate was a mere 3.3 percent. By 1969, it was up to 15.9 percent, which overheated the economy. In 1970 and 1971, it was brought under control at 9 percent. In 1973, it climbed again to 15 percent. The GNP increased from U.S. $2,300 million in 1960 to $9,500 million in 1975. Tony Patrick, "Park Tenses for the Challenge," Far Eastern Economic Review (January 7, 1974): p. 36.

28. Pukhan Ch'ongam (General Handbook on North Korea) (Seoul: Research Institute on Communist Bloc Problems, 1968), p. 269.

29. Due to the impetus provided during the Korean War, the manufacturing capacities of Japanese industries rose by 17.7 percent between March 1950 and March 1951. In 1952, the rate was 17.0 percent and thereafter rose by approximately 10 percent each year. By September 1955, the manufacturing index stood at 192.4, which meant that manufacturing capacity as a whole almost doubled in five and a half years. See Shigeto Tsuru, "Internal Industrial and Business Trends," <u>The Annals of the American Academy of Political and Social Science</u> 308 (November 1956): 88.

30. In his response to the San Francisco Peace Treaty of September 8, 1951, Kim Il-song stated that, "This treaty seeks to expand the aggressive strategy of the U.S. and the U.S. is attempting to utilize the forces of Japanese militarism to infringe on various communist countries including China and the Soviet Union. We cannot overlook the strengthening of the Japanese mainland with U.S. armed forces which is close to Korea with this treaty." Choson Chungang T'ongsihsa (Korean Central News Agency), <u>Choson Chungang Nyongam</u> (The Korean Central Yearbook), 1953, p. 115.

31. Pak Song-ch'ol is reported to have graduated from Sophia University and was a key figure in the organization of the General Federation of Koreans Residing in Japan. Sekai Seikei Chosakai (Research Association for World Political Economies), <u>Kankoku-Hoku Chosen Jinmei Jiten</u> (Biographical Dictionary of South and North Korea) (Tokyo, 1966), p. 194.

32. Prime Minister Miki stated that Japan's experience shows that, "Poverty will be eliminated only when the developing countries are able to educate and train their people and acquire the capital, organization and productive capacity to generate new wealth as self-reliant participants in an interdependent and cooperating world economy." Kazushige Hirasawa, "Japan's Emerging Foreign Policy," <u>Foreign Affairs</u> 54, no. 1 (October 1975): 155-72.

33. Harrison E. Salisbury, <u>To Peking and Beyond: A Report on the New Asia</u> (New York: The New York Times Book Co., 1973), p. 296.

CHAPTER 2

LEADERSHIP AND THE POLITICAL IDEOLOGY OF KIM IL-SONG

THE CULT OF KIM IL-SONG

In the Mansudae Hall in Pyongyang, the capital of the Democratic People's Republic of Korea, at the opening session of the Fifth Congress of the Korean Workers' Party a settled hush of expectancy pervaded in anticipation of the appearance of the "great leader."

> At 9 a.m. Comrade Kim Il-song, the great leader of the 40 million Korean people, peerless patriot, national hero, ever-victorious iron-willed brilliant commander, and the founder and Leader of our Party mounted the platform. Instantly the attendants all rose and broke into stormy applause and cheers "Long live Comrade Kim Il-song, the great Leader!" and "Long live the Workers' Party of Korea!" shaking the hall. All the delegates and observers shouted <u>manse</u> (hurrah) and sent up cheers again and again, choked with emotion when they saw the great Leader. . . .[1]

This is simply one of the manifestations of the cult of Kim Il-song that pervades the national life of North Korea. The scenario, the performance, the responses are all part of the theatrics that have come to mark that cult. There is no doubt about Kim Il-song's belief in the utility of personalized statecraft. It is a belief that has been nurtured in the vast assembly halls of Pyongyang, where there is no truck with moderation or self-doubt. In a country that has little control over the political forces that play upon its fortunes, the assembly hall has been the innermost redoubt of national reassurance and no other national spokesman has ever commanded the presence that Kim Il-song has on its stage. While the paradox that inheres in the statecraft of Kim can be understood as an exercise in self-image, the results of that paradox have often been too costly to accept even within the Communist bloc. On occasion, when Kim has addressed the world as he has his receptive audiences in Pyongyang, crises have resulted. Short of decisive guarantees of swift success by the North Koreans, promising the noninvolvement of Moscow and Peking, it is unlikely that there would be full Sino-Soviet support for an indiscriminate igniting of a second Korean War. Moreover, as long as the spirit of detente persists, incidents such as the seizure of the USS Pueblo or the wanton aerial destruction of the EC-121 are unlikely, without raising grave concerns among friends and foes. The stakes and the risks are far too high to allow vanity and personal political aggrandizement to be the curse of detente among the great powers.

Kim's problems of leadership and statecraft are quite natural. There is an unbridled quality about the political and economic developments that surround and impinge on the DPRK. But, as the spokesman for a country that generates higher expectations than guarantees of national self-realization, Kim Il-song apparently believes that it is necessary for the masses to believe that his leadership will hold at bay or even subdue the forces that threaten to thwart the national goals of Korea.

Kim Il-song's style of leadership combines elements of a Korean authoritarian tradition that has imbued his promethean convictions with the tradition of highly personalized rule enhancing the power of leaders such as Josef Stalin, Mao Tse-tung, and Ho Chi-minh. However, if there are any stellar examples that inspired the creation of the cult of Kim Il-song, they have probably all been surpassed by the deification now being accorded to the great leader in Pyongyang. This is because the theatrics of leadership is part of the national act that must be played out to pry the country loose from old moorings and outmoded beliefs. It is the conviction of the leadership that fears must be dispelled by the undaunted, timidity by heroics, conservatism by progressivism, and egotism by patriotism. The conviction is based on the belief that only total mobilization under a strong leader will bring about the cohesiveness that North Korea needs to unify the country and assert itself internationally. More significantly, Kim Il-song believes that history is on the side of spartan regimes capable of sustaining discipline and sacrifice in the competition with bourgeois imperialist societies, among which imperialism is regarded merely as an extension of a never-ending quest for ungratified appetites.

The exhortation to "live and study like the anti-Japanese partisans" is no idle call, even in this day of rising industrialization and modernization. It is part of the effort to sustain a revolutionary ardor in the face of rising expectations and to give modern day currency to an old spirit that must be kept alive for contemporary political and economic emulation struggles. Kim's efforts to use the past to make the issues of the present appear in sharper relief also reflects his determination to use his own conception of "scientific materialism" to link the evolving new Socialist man in North Korea to the world around him.

While rapid changes in the world that surrounds Korea have been disconcerting to a country that has been struggling against the weight of its own backwardness, recent changes have aided the transformation of Kim Il-song from a pessimist willing to take short-term risks for possible long-run advantages into an optimist who now sees in the triumphs of the North Vietnamese and the Cambodians and the strength of the nations of the Middle East, especially the oil-producing countries, hope for the small countries that at one time seemed to Kim on the verge of being sacrificed at the altar of great power interests. Events such as the Cultural Revolution in China and the bloody border clashes between Russian and Chinese troops, at a time when the fortunes of the small countries were perceived to be hanging in balance because of the war in Vietnam, did little to quiet apprehensions in Pyongyang. Yet, as Kim looks ahead to the ultimate issue of unification, the question remains whether a nation oriented to absolute personal loyalty can cope with the South, which also has yet to find out whether loyalty will be greater to the Pak Chong-hui regime or to the nation if a final showdown were to occur. As Kim and Pak prepare for such an occurrence, the outcome may very well hinge on the age-old Korean problem of achieving maximum national unity in the face of foreign aggression.

THE IDEOLOGICAL COMPONENT

The Hegelian view that placed Asia "outside of the World's history" became an integral part of the Marxian analysis of Oriental society. To the basic Hegelian characterization of Oriental society as "unchanging and stagnant" Marx added his own explanation of the static nature of Asian society "in terms of its unique mode of production, based on common property and giving rise to Oriental despotism."[2]

The Marxian analysis, which posited the "unchanging and stagnant" nature of the "Asiatic mode of production" clearly nullified the dialectic as the mode of negation under which Asiatic societies could suppress themselves, induce contradictions, and set in motion their own negation. By extending the Marxian analysis, it could be argued that since Asian countries such as Korea were incapable of undergoing internal transformation through a dialectical process that would carry them to the stage of capitalism, and since capitalism had to be attained prior to the victory of socialism, it was possible to endorse European colonialism as a necessary phase in the evolution toward socialism. It meant that colonialism was necessary to the world revolution of the proletariat since without such a revolution, Asian countries like Korea would be unable to extricate themselves from what Hegel had referred to as their "unchanging and stagnant" condition.

Like many other Asian revolutionary leaders, Kim Il-song, a self-proclaimed Marxist-Leninist, has had little to say about Marx's analysis of the non-European world. To the restive Korean leadership, the main attraction of Marxism was that it provided promises of a revolutionary way out of economic backwardness and political stagnation. However, while the embrace of Marxism by the North Korean leadership was enthusiastic, the embrace had pragmatic overtones. Over the years, the North Korean leadership has shown little inclination to engage in philosophical debate over deep and potentially awkward ideological issues. Moreover, a promethean attitude and an abiding faith in purposive political activity prevented Kim from being attracted to some of the more clasically oriented Marxist views that stressed the determinism of historical-material forces and that regarded Europe as the cradle of revolution.

Instead, Kim has tended to look upon Marxism as "a mode of scientific analysis for opportune revolutionary conditions."[3] He prefers the aspect of Marxism that makes it "a powerful weapon for revolutionary struggle" as the most relevant and redeeming feature of Marxist ideology in countries such as North Korea. Moreover, he has regarded Leninism as a theory of revolution that "creatively developed and further enriched Marxism to suit the new historical conditions of the era of imperialism and the proletarian revolution."[4]

According to Kim, it was Lenin who made it possible for the underdeveloped Asian countries to enter the mainstream of the proletarian revolution and it was Lenin who was instrumental in breaking down the barriers of "social chauvinism," thereby enabling countries like North Korea to enter the "orbit of historical progress." By implication, the Hegelian and Marxist viewpoints that had placed Asian countries like Korea "outside of world history" and made them simple "objects of history" had been wiped away by Leninism.

Lenin's ideas on the uneven development of capitalism in the age of imperialism raised doubts about the universality of Marxian "laws" governing stages of historical development. But at the same time it led to a theoretical reconciliation with the fact that capitalism was still confined to Western Europe and that by the latter part of the nineteenth century, capitalism was on the move to far reaches of the world as an imperialist force. Imperialism raised the specter of Western encroachment, but in that threat to the underdeveloped countries, Lenin recognized the formidable potentialities for the exploitation of discontent as the source of revolutionary transformation in the backward colonial areas. The Koreans themselves have never lost sight of that fact and from that recognition there emerged an opportunity to restore and reemphasize the original Marxian conception of revolution as an inexorable part of history in spite of the theoretical inconsistencies visited on Marx's laws of history by unforeseen historical developments. For Asian revolutionaries like Kim Il-song, Lenin's update of Marx's theory of capitalism in the era of imperialism provided a prescient melding of theory and practice. It allowed the "exploited" as the backward victims of imperialism to become the main force of the revolution and the Leninist standard bearers of progressivism with bona-fide claims to their own understanding of Marxism-Leninism.

In spite of the nonproletarian antecedents handed down by traditional Korean society, an intercession of ideas that began with Lenin and continued with Trotsky and Stalin enabled a leader like Kim Il-song to lay claim to the creation of a Workers' Party led by a proletarian vanguard. Marx conceived of the "dictatorship of the proletariat" as a form of rule under which the proletariat would exercise leadership through representative bodies as societies underwent a process of transition from capitalism to socialism. So conceived, the dictatorship of the proletariat could be used to destroy the production relations that are the cause of usury and profits. However, Marx had assumed that the proletarian majority would be polarized in relation to the bourgeoisie and that the dictatorship would evolve along class lines and not in terms of the dominance of a political party as conceived later on by Lenin. Under the Leninist formula, the "dictatorship of the proletariat" came to mean the dictatorship of the Communist Party as a vanguard of the proletariat. It meant that although the Party was to be the spokesman for the proletariat and, ultimately, for the entire working class, it was no longer necessary for the Party membership to be of true proletarian origins. Such formulations had a profound impact on leaders like Mao Tse-tung and Kim Il-song.[5]

Kim Il-song believes that a proletarian dictatorship can achieve the realization of an indivisible and unified party entity composed of "the leader, the party, and the masses," and that a party without a leader is like "an army without a commander." He holds that the "creator and overall leadership of the proletarian dictatorship system" is the "leader of the revolution," meaning, presumably, himself. He adds that "the leader" is the "unitary core for the unity and solidarity of the class organizations" and is also the "supreme leader." In the DPRK it is emphasized that Kim Il-song's ideas on the dictatorship of the proletariat "deeply and correctly reflects the requirements of natural law for the development of the revolutionary struggle and for the sake of the great tasks of communism of the working class" and that the ideas represent "a firm guarantee" to uphold the overall victory of the "Korean and world revolutions."[6] In other words, Kim not only sees the dictatorship of the proletariat being exercised by a small vanguard that forms the Party, but he also sees the necessity for himself to be at the forefront of that vanguard. The Leninist belief in self-determination and in the role of the Party as the vanguard of the proletariat provided men like Kim with convenient justifications to personally guide their revolutions.

Moreover, Lenin's belief that the socialist revolution could be victorious "in a few countries or even in a single country" during the new age of imperialistic conflicts and proletarian revolutions may have unwittingly downgraded the leading role of the Soviet or European-centered leadership in Asia. Lenin and Stalin may have expected the communist movement to be centered in Europe or at least led by the Kremlin but, instead, their theoretical formulations allowed Asian leaders like Mao Tse-tung and Kim Il-song to equate their tardy Asian-conceived revolutions and their belated and still backward industrial development with socialism. It also allowed them to stake their claim to preeminence as creators of revolutionary models more suited to the so-called "concrete realities" of the underdeveloped areas of the world where most of the revolutionary ferment can now be found.

Thus, what began originally as a European Marxist view of Asia was abandoned by a line of Kremlin leaders beginning with Lenin and it subsequently evolved into an Asian view of Marxism-Leninism with significant overtones for the future development of Communist doctrine in Asia. In the process, the initiative was passed on to the Asian leadership and in the case of North Korea, when conditions finally permitted, Kim Il-song emerged to lay claim to the originality of his own "creative applications" of Marxist-Leninist principles to conditions in Korea. It was out of that condition that chuche,* the national component, began to emerge in North Korea.

---

*In the past, the North Korean media tended to translate the term as "self-identity" or "national identity," but recently, perhaps for the lack of a truly adequate translation or for nationalistic reasons, the transliterated form has been used exclusively.

THE NATIONAL COMPONENT

According to a major North Korean source, chuche refers to an outlook that insists on a "thorough defense of the viewpoint of masters relating to the revolution of one's own country."[7] It argues for the creative application of the principles of Marxism-Leninism to the "concrete realities" of the country and for the masters of the Korean revolution to adopt "resolute viewpoints and independent ideas" that properly belong to the Korean Workers' Party and the Korean people. It calls for the complete submission of all efforts required to successfully accomplish the tasks of the revolution to the Korean viewpoint. It recognizes the importance of Marxist-Leninist principles and is emphatic in the assertion that both considerations must be tailored to conditions in Korea. It deemphasizes "the revolution of other countries" and emphasizes total concern for the Korean revolution and that a "national identity" reflective of that concern must be integral to the party's ideological activities. Therefore, all ideological activities must invariably be subordinate to the viewpoint of the Korean Workers' Party. Finally, chuche positively rejects "a mechanical interpretation of Marxism-Leninism" and the revolutionary lessons of other countries unless they can be applied to conditions in Korea.

A heavy overlay of nationalism is also expressed in the rejection of "dogmatism, formalism, and national nihilism, which disregards all of the superior traditions and national inheritances" of the Korean people.[8] North Korean accounts emphasize that the mainsprings of North Korea's ideological beliefs emerged from the revolutionary experiences of the Korean communists themselves. In doing so, they have exalted the role of the Koreans while ignoring the contributions of the USSR and the PRC to Korea's revolutionary cause.

The term chuche obviously carries special connotations for Koreans.[9] The conventional dictionary definition of the term is "subjective." But the term has been particularly meaningful in times of national political duress when subjectivity was regarded as a right among Koreans suffering what they regarded as national oppression. The term carries an intuitive and very private identity that seems to express a shared consciousness of "being" rather than a concrete idea that can clearly be committed to words. In turning it into a political shibboleth, Kim Il-song has clearly gauged the worth of the term as a symbol of shared identity.

The relationship of chuche to foreign policy has been expressed as such by Kim Il-song: ". . . the Government of the Republic formulates its foreign policy on the basis of the chuche idea and is guided by this idea in carrying out its external activities. In a word, our Republic firmly maintains its independence in its foreign activities."[10]

The key word in that statement is "independence." According to Kim, "Independence is what keeps a man alive. If he loses independence in society, he cannot be called a man; he differs little from an animal." He adds that, "For our people today, there is no more pressing matter than to drive out foreign aggressors and establish national sovereignty throughout the country."[11]

Kim notes that the "progressive people" of the world "want" to live in accordance with the chuche idea. In making that point, Kim alludes to the problems of his own country and other Socialist countries in dealing with great power intrusions. "To say nothing of the socialist countries, the newly independent countries also oppose interference and restrictions by other countries and are taking the road of independence and self-sustenance. Even capitalist countries do not want to blindly follow big countries any longer. . . ."[12]

It is in the context of "independence" that Kim has claimed universality for his ideas on chuche. However, too often, Pyongyang's ideas about independent action took the form of exporting advice on violence and internal subversion. Such programs have run counter to North Korean statements of principle under chuche to respect the principle of noninterference in the internal affairs of other countries. In countries like Mexico, the violence of terrorists trained by the North Koreans retarded normal efforts to inspire trust in its diplomatic program for "aid and assistance." It is for that reason that chuche has enjoyed more practical currency at home than abroad.

Initially, the term chuche enjoyed very little public currency. One of the main reasons was probably that from August 1945, when Soviet units marched into Pyongyang, until 1958, when the Chinese People's Volunteers departed for home, North Korea was under the constant scrutiny and protection of foreign troops on home soil and there was little sense in forcefully articulating the idea of chuche publicly.

It was only after the departure of foreign troops from North Korea and the evolution of the Communist bloc from what was once assumed to be a monolith into a system troubled by polycentric tendencies that conditions began to emerge for such potentially contentious ideas as chuche.

However, the applications of chuche have not been without paradox. Too often, the difference between ideals and reality has been a measure of a more fundamental clash between reason and naked power. For the North Koreans, the problem has not only been one of finding an authentic Korean identity. It has also involved finding their place in a precarious and unpredictable world order. Both Marx and Engels had envisaged the possibility of a new order to replace bourgeois society with its "classes and class antagonisms" and the evolution of a system under which "the free development of each" would be "the condition for the free development of all."[13] Unfortunately, this has not always been the case even under the ideals of proletarian internationalism. According to North Korean accounts, built-in inequalities have always been present. "Needless to say, national inequality as well as class distinctions should be eradicated to build socialism and communism. Yet, this inequality does not disappear as soon as the socialist revolution triumphs in each country, nor does it vanish through amalgamation of nations in this or that way."[14]

There is also that paradox inherent in the vehement North Korean insistence that there should be "no high party and low party" within the Communist bloc, especially as authoritarian pressures have come to bear on Pyongyang's national interests and ideals.

The principle derivatives of chuche are not Marxist principles but elements that stem from a deeply Korean social and political order. The reasons underlying the practical applications of chuche must also be examined within the context of a rapidly changing international order that continues to confront Pyongyang with the age-old issue of whether North Korea's destinies are to be shaped at home or await the force of external circumstances. To move in that direction, it has been necessary to establish a link between (what Kim has referred to as) "Korean things" with Marxism. In the early stages of the DPRK Kim complained of cadres who knew Marxist theory but knew nothing of Korean history or those who were well read in Korean classics but lacked sufficient knowledge in Marxist theory.[15] Chuche now seems to represent a more confident viewpoint.

The heavy emphasis that Kim Il-song has placed on the Korean "viewpoint" in chuche has often made the concept seem highly defensive in an offensive sort of way. It represents the sum and substance of what may be characterized as the Korean bias that has often made the logic of a Korean stand on foreign issues seem so solid and even bellicose to the outside world. It is that very facet of chuche that Kim has turned to political purposes in articulating national objectives and marshaling popular support.

THE NATURE OF THE POLICY MECHANISM

The reigning figure in the formulation of both foreign and domestic policy in North Korea is Kim Il-song. The sources of his influence over policy are institutional and personal.

The responsibility for the formulation of policy rests with the Political Committee of the Central Committee of the Korean Workers' Party. It is the domain of the North Korean political elite and it is the source of the institutional influence that Kim wields as the presiding leader within that group. Without firsthand observation, the workings of the policy mechanism must be left to conjecture but some indications show it to be less a forum than a legitimizing agent at this point.[16] One reason is that Kim's inordinate political power makes the Political Committee an unlikely place for any committee member to seek a personal showdown with Kim on any sensitive issue. It would probably be much more effective to lobby for a particular point of view prior to the final vote within the Political Committee. Second, the increasing complexity of events and issues makes it impossible for the leadership to properly reconcile their generalist views with the abstractions that usually inhere in the events and crises that they are called upon to cope with. The support of specialists who are capable of clearly laying out the options is necessary. It is the specialists and the "functionaries" concerned who must perform the staff work that will cut through the bureaucratic maze to move the decision-making process toward the consensus that will obviate any wrangling once it is taken into the Political Committee for a vote.

The monolithic character of the policy mechanism can be attributed to the dominance of Kim Il-song and to the assertiveness with which policy is implemented in North Korea. The purge, as an instrument of policy, also seems to have contributed to that view.

The purge seems to have served three basic purposes. First, to enhance the personal power of Kim Il-song. Second, to eliminate dissidence as a source of disunity and as a focal point of foreign lobbying. Third, to infuse the leadership with new blood in recent years.

In the initial stage, at least five major factions became targets of the purge.[17] One major target was the nationalist faction headed by Cho Man-sik. Cho, a nationalist and a man of established credentials as a leader, made Kim seem boorish by comparison and had to be eliminated. With the connivance of the Soviet Occupation Command, Cho was removed from public life in January 1946 for his alleged opposition to the great power trusteeship plan for Korea.

The second faction to be purged was the domestic faction. The major figure in that faction, Hyon Chun-hyok, advocated a nationalistic brand of Communist ideology and was not averse to supporting a republican form of democratic government headed by Cho Man-sik. Hyon was assassinated in Pyongyang in September 1945. Chu Nyong-ha, another prominent leader of the domestic faction, became the pawn in a scheme to expose two other prominent members of the faction despised by Kim Il-song and the Soviet command. Chu was later purged as a "factionalist." O Ki-sop, whose prominence as a theoretician and as the dominant figure in the domestic faction that controlled areas around North and South Hamgyong Provinces, became too influential and was also purged.

The third faction to be purged was the South Korean Workers' Party faction. That faction, which was headed by Pak Hon-yong, was the most tightly knit of the factions and therefore represented the most formidable threat to the ascendancy of the Kim Il-song faction. Pak's elimination was part of a thorough liquidation of the ranks of that faction and Pak's demise was based on accusations that included consorting and cooperating with the "imperialists" and profiting from public property.

The Soviet faction was the fourth faction to be purged. Ho Ka-i, a noted and experienced political organizer with organizational skills and aversion to Kim Il-song's crudity and penchant for what he regarded as mediocrity, alarmed the Kim faction. On charges of willfulness, favoritism, and the dilution of Party ranks with impure elements, Ho too was purged. Kim Yol, who was also highly regarded by his Soviet mentors and who, like Ho Ka-i, enjoyed easy access to the Soviet Occupation Command, was disliked by Kim for his arrogance and condescension and for his antipathy toward the Kim faction. Kim Yol was convicted of embezzlement, rape, and anti-Party crimes.

The fifth faction to be purged was the Chinese or Yenan faction. The most famous of that group was Mu Chong. Mu was reportedly regarded highly by Mao Tse-tung and was a former division commander in the Chinese Eighth Route Army. Mu Chong was contemptuous of Soviet efforts to prop up Kim and was finally purged on charges drawn against him during the Korean War. Mu reportedly disobeyed Kim Il-song's orders to defend Pyongyang to the very last after Kim himself had retreated into Manchuria. Pak Il-u, another former member of the Eighth Route Army who also joined Mu Chong in harboring contempt for the Kim faction expanded his influence as an authority in police systems. Eventually he headed the security system for all of North Korea, which probably made him a threat. Pak was also purged.

The early factional struggles and purges were power struggles that led to the political consolidation of Kim Il-song. Kim's cause was served by the presence of the Soviet occupation command (which was apparently under orders from the Kremlin to place Kim in power), by the availability of sufficient personal support from members of his faction to allow him to withstand the challenge of other factions, and, finally, by the highly divided state of the opposition where opportunism and a concern for personal advancement tended to override factional goals and play into the hands of the Kim Il-song faction.

Two major events marked the final consolidation of Kim Il-song's position at the top of the North Korean hierarchy. The purge of Vice Premier and Minister of Foreign Affairs Pak Hon-yong and 12 of his followers from the domestic faction in August 1953, and the purge between August 1956 and March 1958 of Vice Premier and

Minister of Machine Industry, Pak Ch'ang-ok, Vice Premier Ch'oe Ch'ang-ik, and the Chairman of the Presidium of the Supreme People's Assembly, Kim Tu-pong. The removal of Pak Ch'ang-ok of the Soviet faction and Ch'oe Ch'ang-ik and Kim Tu-pong of the Chinese faction plus the withdrawal of the Chinese People's Volunteers from North Korea finally set the stage for Kim to begin scaffolding his own regime. Speaking of that period, Kim stated that: "The August 1956 Plenum and the Party Conference in March 1958 particularly enabled the Party to root all anti-Party factional elements out of its ranks and attain a great victory in the struggle for its unity and solidarity."[18]

While the self-serving quality of Kim Il-song's statecraft is clearly manifested in his political cult, it is also evident that Kim was concerned about the damage that the factionalists had inflicted on the North Korean movement. In large measure, the evolution of the cult can be traced to that condition. However, in fostering the cult, Kim placed himself in a dilemma that became increasingly troublesome in the late 1960s. By making his thoughts infallible, Kim may have undermined the credibility of the Party as the supreme authority.[19]

The roots of that dilemma can be traced to the very nature of the cult of Kim Il-song. Factionalism was and apparently still is endemic to North Korean politics. The political response to that condition represented one facet of the cult. From Kim's standpoint, the opposition simply had to be liquidated. Second, efforts have been made to supplant old ideas with Marxist-Leninist ideology but Kim has maintained symbolic trappings of a bygone era to lend substance to his paternalistic style of leadership.[20] To completely dispense with elements of an authoritarian Korean tradition would be un-Korean and even counterproductive. Finally, he has also availed himself of the tradition of personalized rule established by men like Mao and Stalin, and has recognized the political utility of the cult. In Mao Tse-tung's case, the cult was used during the Great Proletarian Cultural Revolution to regain the political power that had been lost previously. Kim Il-song never had the misfortune to lose the reins of power. Like Stalin, once his enemies were destroyed, Kim used the cult to consolidate his political power. Once the cult was underway, it fed on new sources of power.

The "strengthened unity and solidarity" of the Party and the "complete unity" of the Communist movement in Korea, all of which began with the emergence of the cult, have been regarded by Kim as the "most precious achievements" of the Korean communists. It was a fundamental condition that Kim felt had to be attained before he could turn with confidence to the foreign relations of the DPRK.

NOTES

1. Pyongyang Times, November 3, 1970, p. 1.
2. Marx was struck by the fragmenting effect that the immense waterworks of the Orient had on Asiatic society. Kim Il-song unwittingly referred to this phenomenon once when he stated that, "The peasant and handicraftsmen lack a collective spirit and an organizational capacity because they are scattered and live individually." Nodong Sinmun, March 5, 1975. The most extensive discussion on the Asiatic mode of production can be found in Karl A. Wittfogel, Oriental Despotism: A Comparative Study of Total Power (New Haven: Yale University Press, 1957). See also, Shlomo Avineri, ed., Karl Marx on Colonialism and Modernization (New York: Doubleday, 1968), pp. 10-11.
3. Ch'olhak Sajon (Dictionary of Philosophy) (Pyangyang: DPRK Academy of Social Sciences Publishing House, 1970), p. 227.
4. Kim Il-song, "The Great Idea of Lenin on the National Liberation Struggle in Colonies in the East is Triumphing," Korean Youths and Students, no. 106, 1970, p. 2. The article was also carried in the April 16, 1970 issue of Pravda.
5. Stuart R. Schram, The Political Thought of Mao Tse-tung (New York: Praeger, 1969), p. 60. Kim argues that the late emergence of the Korean proletariat from economic backwardness under the Yi Dynasty and colonial rule under Japan has made the Korean working class a more "pure class" than West European classes with "centuries of history." Yi Ch'ong-won, Struggle in Korea for Proletarian Hegemony (Pyongyang: DPRK Academy of Sciences, 1955), p. 145.
6. Ch'olhak Sajon, p. 642.
7. Taejung Chongch'i Yongo Sajon (Dictionary of Mass Political Terminology) (Pyongyang: Korean Workers' Party Publishing House, 1964), p. 169. A discussion on the fundamentals of chuche is also contained in Hyongmyong ui Widaehan Suryong Kim Il-song Tongji ui Chuche Sasang (The Chuche Idea of the Great Leader of the Revolution Comrade Kim Il-song) (Pyongyang: DPRK Academy of Social Sciences Publishing House, 1972), pp. 3-15.
8. Ibid.
9. The term is also used in South Korea where it is usually referred to as chuchesong. The suffix song can be translated as making it "chuche-ness." According to one source, it means "to solidify the consciousness of cohesion, uniqueness, and belongingness of the nation as a social organism to meet the challenges of other nations." Yim Seong-hi, "Thoughts of the Times," Korea Times, September 15, 1972, p. 2.

10. Kim Il-song, "On Some Problems of Our Party's Chuche Idea and the DPRK Government's Internal and External Policies," Pyongyang Times, September 23, 1972.

11. Ibid.

12. Ibid.

13. Karl Marx and Friedrich Engels, The Communist Manifesto, trans. by Samuel Moore, ed. by Joseph Katz (New York: Washington Square Press, 1967), p. 95.

14. "Embodiment of Comrade Kim Il-song's Great Idea of Chuche is the Guarantee for Victory of our Revolution," Korea Today, no. 143 (Pyongyang: Foreign Languages Publishing House, 1968), p. 15.

15. Kim Il-song, Selected Works, vol. 1 (Pyongyang: Foreign Languages Publishing House, 1965), pp. 293-94.

16. Robert A. Scalapino and Chong-Sik Lee, Communism in Korea, vol. 2 (Berkeley: University of California Press, 1972), p. 726.

17. There is a rich source of information on factional alignments and factional struggles in ibid. Other sources include Kim Ch'ang-sun, Fifteen-Year History of North Korea, U.S. Joint Publications Research Service, JPRS: 18,925, April 26, 1963; and U.S. U.S. Joint Publications Research Service, History of Factional Rivalry in North Korea, JPRS, March 12, 1964.

18. Kim, Selected Works, op. cit., vol. 2, p. 225.

19. In the late 1960s the cult was balanced by emphasizing the unitary ideology (yuil sasang) of the Party and in late 1973 by emphasizing loyalty to the "Party center" (tang chungang) while emphasizing supreme loyalty to Kim Il-song.

20. The North Koreans constantly refer to Kim Il-song as the "paternal leader" (oboi suryong) and even as the "fatherly Marshal" (aboji wonsu).

CHAPTER

3

THE IMPACT OF STALIN AND STALINISM: 1945-53

Paramount Soviet influence in North Korea began and ended with Stalin. Aside from Lenin, no other leader has received the acclaim that Stalin has in North Korea.[1] Government operations in North Korea began under Soviet military administration and by the time the Democratic People's Republic of Korea was inaugurated on September 9, 1948, the cold war and the American-Soviet confrontation were well underway. It was a time of complete relisnce on the Kremlin. However, when the Korean War broke out, it set in motion a chain of events that were to disrupt the patron-client relationship that had come to govern relations between Moscow and Pyongyang. The Chinese impact in Korea was to break unwittingly the lock that Stalin had clamped on the levers of political control in the DPRK. For China, the decision to enter the war was largely for reasons of national security.[2] But the war created conditions that enabled Kim to cast off the fetters of a puppet and finally allow nationalism and his penchant for personal political aggrandizement to loom as his guide for political action.

THE INITIAL STAGE OF DIPLOMACY

The pattern of diplomacy that first emerged in the DPRK was indicative of the predominant Soviet influence. The situation that prevailed in Eastern Europe after World War II as a result of the disproportionate power wielded by the USSR over the region was also prevalent in large measure in North Korea. Kim Il-song needed Stalin's support to confront the West and to win over the people of North Korea. Up until 1945, Kim was virtually unknown at home or abroad.[3] In return for primary Soviet influence, Stalin was willing to build Kim a political base and a national image.

On October 12, 1948, the USSR became the first country to establish diplomatic relations with the DPRK. Three days later, Mongolia followed suit and within a week, Poland and Czechoslovakia established diplomatic relations with Pyongyang. Then, in November 1948, Rumania, Hungary, and Bulgaria extended diplomatic recognition to the DPRK.[4] Significantly, all six countries that joined with the Soviet Union in establishing diplomatic relations with the DPRK were Soviet satellites. In 1949, three countries, Albania, China, and East Germany, extended diplomatic recognition (in that order) to North Korea. On January 31, 1950, North Vietnam opened diplomatic relations with North Korea and it was approximately ten years before Pyongyang's diplomacy was extended beyond that small circle of nations.[5]

The primacy of Soviet influence, which was evident in the pattern of DPRK diplomacy, was due to adroit Soviet planning and execution. Soviet planning apparently began well in advance of the end of World War II. According to one observer, the Soviet Comintern School to train postwar leaders of the satellite countries included a group of Koreans who were being trained in secrecy in a building on their training grounds that was fenced off and placed off-limits to every trainee in the school. Secrecy had to be maintained because the Soviet Union was still a signatory to the nonaggression pact that it had concluded with Japan, and the Koreans were being prepared for the takeover of Korea, which was then occupied by Japan.[6]

On August 9, 1945, three days after the dropping of the first atomic bomb on Hiroshima and just five days prior to the final Japanese surrender that brought World War II to an end, the Soviet Union declared war on Japan.[7] Within days, Soviet forces were on their way to occupy North Korea.

The Soviet policy in North Korea was to establish an indigenous political regime that would be responsive to Soviet influence. The DPRK was expected to be "independent," at least to the extent of being a self-sufficient regime. Initially, the plan proceeded smoothly because the progress achieved at each stage coincided with the perceived expectations of both Moscow and Pyongyang. As events were to bear out years later, Moscow's perception of Korean "independence" was to remain largely figurative, while Pyongyang adopted a literal interpretation of the term. Initially, however, after 35 years of foreign domination, the Korean leaders were willing to bide their time and trade on the opportunities offered by the Kremlin.

The Soviet Occupation Command immediately established a People's Democracy on the foundations of an existing nationwide network of people's committees.[8] They then proceeded to erect an official government mechanism with all the trappings of a modern republic. Like the Soviet model, from which it was derived, it was harnessed to the policy mechanism of the Korean Workers' Party. The entire scheme was apparently the brainchild of Stalin, who arranged to place Kim Il-song in power.[9] Armed with ready access to the Party core, Stalin was able to wield considerable influence over North Korean affairs.

The pattern of diplomacy that emerged out of Pyongyang soon after the Soviet recognition of the DPRK can be attributed to those arrangements. It served at least two purposes. Under the aegis of the Soviet Union, it provided the DPRK with legitimate diplomatic recognition within the Communist bloc. Second, by preserving a facade of Korean independence, the Soviets were able to cloak their manipulation of the political process in the DPRK. Under those arrangements, it is difficult to conceive of Soviet noninvolvement in the preparations that led to the Korean War.

PRELUDE TO THE KOREAN WAR

By the end of World War II, conditions had shifted markedly in favor of the Soviet Union on the European continent. The conditions fit in well with the Kremlin's plan to solve the problem of outside aggression by establishing friendly satellite states along its borders. Fortunately for Stalin, the traditional preoccupation with security that colored the psychology of the Soviet leadership was matched in intensity by the concern for national security harbored by the North Korean leadership. Therefore, when the vanguard units of the Soviet Army first marched into Pyongyang, the issue of Korean independence bore a more immediate and practical relationship to the issue of Soviet hegemony in Korea than to the ideals and aspirations of the Soviet-trained Korean leaders. Stalin's main concern was the "eastern flank" of the socialist camp to be defended by a self-sustaining North Korean regime friendly and responsive to the Soviet Union.

One of the major consequences of Stalin's unwillingness to collaborate in establishing joint controls over divided nations like Germany and Korea was the U.S. initiative to conclude a peace treaty with Japan even without Soviet concurrence. The reversal of the U.S. occupation policy in Japan was a result of the rapidly deteriorating condition in China for the Nationalists and the consequent U.S. belief that a hostile China would require a stronger Japanese presence in Asia. The threat as seen by the Kremlin was that a peace treaty would inevitably lead to Japanese rearmament. According to George F. Kennan, it was the perception of just such a threat that compelled Moscow to "unleash the attack" that opened the Korean War.[10] A major response to the new threat raised by the proposed American-Japanese rapprochement was the establishment of a Sino-Soviet alliance on February 14, 1950.

There were favorable overtones to the Sino-Soviet Treaty that bode well for both signatories. For China, it meant an instant elevation to a position of near parity with the Soviet Union in the Socialist camp. The arrangement contrasted sharply with the satellite status forced on the East European regimes by the Kremlin. It also produced a joint contingency arrangement in response to the threat of the U.S. rearmament in Japan, which was becoming increasingly ominous to the Chinese.[11]

From the Soviet standpoint, the treaty significantly reduced the chances for an American role in mainland China. Up to that point, diplomatic relations between China and the United States had been a distinct possibility. Had diplomatic relations been established between the two nations, it would have raised further implications for Soviet national security with a U.S. presence in China. The Kremlin could hardly have countenanced such a development in view of its existing fear of an American-West German threat in Europe and the possibility of an American-Japanese threat in the Far East. Actually, the Korean War did represent a strategic Soviet response to conditions attaining on its Asian front just as the Berlin blockade was its response to strategic considerations perceived on its European front.

As for the decision to ignite the war, the prospects for a Northern invasion of the ROK were promising on a number of counts. The withdrawal of U.S. military troops from the ROK was followed by other developments that seemed to indicate an American indifference to the defense of South Korea. A growing mood of economic and military commitment to Western Europe was not balanced by a counterpart mood of support for U.S. initiatives in Asia.[12]

Moreover, Soviet intentions may have been unwittingly encouraged in 1949 when a statement by General MacArthur appeared to leave South Korea out of the so-called "U.S. defense perimeter." Although Secretary of State Dean Acheson's speech at the National Press Club on January 12, 1950, followed the outline of General MacArthur's defense line and although that indication was regarded by critics as being the sign of U.S. passivity which encouraged the subsequent North Korean invasion of the South, the U.S. interest in the defense of South Korea was thought to have been covered in subsequent paragraphs of that speech. According to Acheson:

> So far as the military security of other areas of the Pacific is concerned, it must be clear that no person can guarantee these areas against military attack. . . . Should such an attack occur . . . the initial reliance must be on the people attacked to resist it and then upon the commitments of the entire civilized world under

IMPACT OF STALINISM 37

> the Charter of the United Nations, which so far
> has not proved a weal reed to lean on by any
> people who are determined to protect their in-
> dependence against outside aggression.[13]

However, because political cohesiveness was suspect in Seoul and because the infant ROK military establishment was ill-equipped and inexperienced, the Soviet advisers in Pyongyang may have been convinced that a swift takeover of the South was possible without too much risk. In other words, the "initial reliance" that Secretary of State Acheson referred to may have been all that the North Koreans thought they needed.[14] Second, Acheson's faith in the UN may have been countered by Soviet cynicism about the UN's ability to mount any kind of military effort. The obstructions caused by the Soviet veto during Security Council deliberations had already been well demonstrated.

Therefore, it could very well have been that when Jacob Malik began the Soviet boycott of the UN Security Council in January 1950, the Kremlin actions were based on three considerations. First, without the U.S. military presence in the ROK, the military victory of the North over the South would be swift and decisive. Second, the impotence of the UN would preclude any decisive outside intervention in Korea. Third, Soviet confidence was justified even to the point of abdicating its veto power in the Security Council with Malik's symbolic pro-Peking boycott against the seating of Taiwan's T. F. Tsiang as China's UN delegate. The Soviet boycott occurred just as Mao and Stalin were putting the final touches to the Sino-Soviet treaty that was signed on February 14, 1950. Ultimately, the strategy played into the hands of the United States since it was Malik's absence from the Security Council that allowed the rest of the Council membership to quickly support the U.S. proposal for a military intervention in Korea soon after the North launched its attack on June 25, 1950.

THE KOREAN WAR AND THE AFTERMATH

The North Korean invasion nearly succeeded. The swift southward advance carried all the way to Pusan before it was finally blunted. On September 15, 1950, General MacArthur ordered an amphibious launching at Inchon, which caught the North Korean forces by surprise just as a UN counteroffensive began out of the Pusan perimeter. The tide of battle quickly shifted in favor of the UN forces and by October 1, the ROK forces were able to cross over the thirty-eighth parallel into North Korea. It was only the entry of the Chinese People's Volunteers (CPV) that prevented a total collapse of the DPRK.

The entry of the CPV into Korea drastically altered the premises of Pyongyang's foreign relations. The most significant impact was on the Kremlin's military leverage in Pyongyang. Much of Stalin's thinking on the initial gamble to allow the war to start was predicated on a need to assuage his pride over the failure of the Berlin blockade and his failure to prevent the formation of NATO.[15] Stalin had counted on a lightning Soviet-supported military victory in Korea followed by a Chinese invasion of Taiwan. On paper there were reasons to believe that the conditions were ripe for a two-pronged assault.[16] The unexpectedly swift UN intervention and the subsequent deterioration of military conditions for the North Koreans after the landing at Inchon and the simultaneous UN counteroffensive necessitated a hasty change in strategy in both Moscow and Peking.

The entry of the CPV into the war saved the DPRK. For Mao Tse-tung, the complex considerations that entered into the decision to intervene in the war included China's proprietary interest in North Korea as a buffer state situated along its Manchurian border.[17] Stalin's overall plan may also have included conceding Mao the leading role in Southeast Asia in return for his own leading role in Northeast Asia.[18]

The costs of military intervention were high for Mao and the PRC. The war exacted a heavy toll on Chinese manpower and materiel at a critical stage in the national reconstruction and development of the PRC and Mao Tse-tung suffered the personal loss of his son in the fighting in Korea.[19] Perhaps an abiding recognition of the personal loss to Mao is implied in frequent references made by the North Korean media during Korean War anniversary observances to the assistance rendered by the Chinese who sent their "finest sons and daughters" to aid the Korean people.

Moreover, on June 27, 1950, an announcement by President Truman, which in effect committed the U.S. Seventh Fleet to the defense of Taiwan, immediately ended Chinese hopes for the "liberation" of Taiwan. Also, following the entry of the CPV into the war, Chinese options concerning the Korean question and the Taiwan question within the UN became increasingly tied to their military position in Korea. Initially, heady tactical victories, especially in November and December 1950, allowed Mao Tse-tung to reject all cease-fire proposals. China's stand enabled the United States to maneuver a UN General Assembly condemnation of China as an aggressor in February 1951 and a subsequent vote in May urged all UN members to refrain from shipping strategic materials to China. In the spring of 1951, heavy American and ROK "killer" attacks began to wreak devastation on the Chinese and North Korean forces and by that summer, China was forced to accede to negotiations without assurances of an American withdrawal from Taiwan or its own admission into the UN.

However, there were also political gains registered by the Chinese side in Korea. The Chinese were undoubtedly mindful of the manner in which the postwar entry of the Yenan contingent of Koreans into Korea was delayed in 1945 by the Soviet command to allow Soviet dominance to be established beforehand in Pyongyang. Therefore, when the CPV arrived in force in 1950, they managed quickly to turn the tables on the Soviet command.[20] Up until then, even North Korean military orders were being initiated by Soviet military advisers.[21] The North Koreans were apparently quite aware of the deep-seated animosities that were being manifested between the Russians and the Chinese as early as 1945 in Korea.

For the North Korean leadership, the entry of the CPV into Korea raised the prospect of a Chinese neutralization of Soviet influence in Pyongyang. But there were also indications of Korean-Chinese friction. Most notable was the alleged conflict between Peng Teh-huai and Kim Il-song. Among the allegations marshaled to bring about the downfall of Peng Teh-huai in Peking years after the end of the Korean War was the following:

> While in Korea, Peng Teh-huai brought big-nation chauvinism into play and raged at Kim Il-song. Said he: "During the period of the War of Resistance, I was Deputy Commander-in-Chief of the 8th Route Army, while Kim Il-song was a puppet division commander of the allied army against Japan." This strained Sino-Korean relations and enabled Soviet revisionism to crawl through the crack.[22]

In order to avoid embroiling themselves in the domestic affairs of China, the North Koreans avoided commenting on Peng Teh-huai, but it is noteworthy that Peng's name is not mentioned at all in the history of the Korean War that was published in Pyongyang.[23]

Following the war, the continued presence of the CPV in Korea and a number of broad developments contributed to a growing coalescence of Korean and Chinese interests.

The Korean War produced economic repercussions in both countries. Both countries were in need of extensive economic rehabilitation. However, while other underdeveloped countries were benefiting from Western aid, the North Koreans and Chinese gradually began to chafe at the restrictive provisions of Soviet aid. The state to which conditions deteriorated in later years was reflected in complaints emanating from Pyongyang.

> . . . [Y]ou furnished us with equipment, stainless steel plates, and other materials at prices

much higher than the world market prices and took away from us scores of tons of gold, quantities of valuable non-ferrous metal and raw materials at prices much lower than the world market prices. Would it not be a reasonable attitude when you talk about your aid to us to mention also that you took valuable materials produced by our people through arduous labor in the most difficult days of our life?[24]

Furthermore, the developments coincided with stepped-up Soviet-aid projects to countries like Egypt and India on terms more favorable than those offered to the beleaguered Chinese and the North Koreans, who found their own terms of payment with the Soviet Union tied to scarce commodities and hard currency.

Throughout that period, however, the North Korean media continued to give equal billing in their press coverage to Soviet and Chinese contributions to the DPRK.

THE INITIAL LIMITS OF CHINESE INFLUENCE IN PYONGYANG

The postwar ascendancy of Chinese influence in the DPRK was not accompanied by a corresponding decline in Soviet influence. Despite the fact that direct military involvement had raised the popularity of the Chinese, the USSR remained as the dominant force of the Communist bloc and the most logical source of military and economic assistance for both the Chinese and the Koreans. Moreover, the entry of the CPV into the war eroded Stalin's overall military control in Korea but it did not damage his credibility with Kim Il-song.

Three basic considerations favored Stalin. First of all, whereas China's revolution was an indigenous, grass roots revolution, North Korea's revolution was a revolution engineered from the top by Stalin. Soviet assistance was instrumental in establishing the DPRK a year prior to the founding of the PRC. Second, although the North Koreans fought under the Chinese Communist Party in Manchuria, they were too far removed from China's Party centers to be influenced markedly by Maoist doctrines.[25] Third, Stalinism struck a responsive chord in Kim. Kim has always believed in industry and autarky as shortcuts to economic well-being. He has believed in agriculture as the bedrock of economic sustenance and capitalization. He has willingly applied terrorism as the ultimate melder of pieties. Finally, he too sees himself as a living legend destined to provide the ultimate symbol of national unity.

IMPACT OF STALINISM

The lure of Stalinism was in its promises of power--a power that could be used to bend Marxism-Leninism to national purposes. Power consolidation in the Stalinist mode meant that the possibilities for national usurpation lay only a step ahead. Both the Chinese and Koreans were early proponents of self-reliance and when the choice of alternative strategies emerged, Kim Il-song, like Stalin before him, opted for priority reliance on heavy industry and agriculture as prescriptions to cure North Korea's underdevelopment. Whether it made sense or not was of secondary importance. Nationalism was the primary consideration and on that score, Kim could at least count on the understanding of Stalin and Mao. Kim's affinity for the twin elements of power and nationalism has always been evident.

> The question of power is the fundamental question in the revolution and the vital question on which the victory of the revolution and the success of constructive work depends. The working class can achieve complete class and national liberation and win in the cause of socialism and communism only when it takes power firmly into its hands, constantly enhances its functions and roles and steadily strengthens the dictatorship of the proletariat.[26]

However, the limits of Chinese influence were also symptomatic of significant changes that were taking place even then to limit Soviet influence over domestic affairs in North Korea.

In Korea, it had been evident from the beginning that a shared dedication to Marxism-Leninism was not compelling enough to foster a shared perception of values between the Russians, the Chinese, and the Koreans. As in the 1920s, when Stalin's view of the China problem from the vantage point of Moscow proved erroneous, his perception of the situation in Korea was also clouded by distance and the unexpected train of events that led to the entry of the Chinese into Korea. Also, the respect that Stalin enjoyed was not transferable to the Soviet operatives in Korea. For tactical and perhaps ethnocentric reasons, the Chinese preferred to keep everyone, including the Russians, in the dark about their own operations. Once a mutual suspicion and a wary preoccupation with each other became endemic to Sino-Soviet relations in Korea, it gave the Koreans a chance to toy with diverse options.

Therefore, although Chinese influence did not supplant Soviet influence immediately, it at least opened the way for a new balance in Korea. It also opened the way for the Chinese to offer viable Asian alternatives to Russian ideas in the DPRK.

Meanwhile, Kim was apparently convinced that he was still Stalin's man and was undeterred by his own wartime humiliation. By 1952, Kim was using the lull in the fighting and the preoccupation of the Chinese with their fight-talk strategy to regain the political initiative by blaming others for North Korea's military setbacks. Pak Hon-yong and Yi Sung-yop were prominent members of the native faction purged on charges of abetting the enemy and for wrongfully overestimating the revolutionary potential in the South. By doing so, Kim not only transferred the onus of his own failures to the South Korean faction, he also eliminated the most able and prestigious leaders who had actually waged the only Communist movement in Korea under Japanese occupation.

Moreover, just as the purge of Ho Ka-i removed a valuable Soviet conduit into the North Korean bureaucracy, the elimination of the popular and pro-Chinese Mu Chong deprived the Chinese of a voice in the Korean military. But Kim was too clever to succumb to the temptation of replacing purged dissidents with nothing but pro-Kim supporters. Instead, he selected native, pro-Soviet, as well as pro-Chinese, replacements who could be influenced, controlled, or watched over by trusted supporters. By doing so, Kim not only consolidated his own power but he was also able to begin closing off potential trouble spots for the entrance of "foreign influences."

At the end of the war, the DPRK was able to renew its relationships with other countries of the bloc. Material aid poured in from many quarters of the Communist bloc. The list was headed by the Soviet Union, which provided 1,000 million rubles worth of gratuitous aid, followed by 800 million yuan of aid from China. Other countries included Poland, which provided 383 million rubles; Czechoslovakia with 440 million rubles, of which 130 million was gratuitous aid; East Germany with 54 million rubles, plus 18 million rubles of technology and equipment; Rumania with 65 million rubles, plus 25 million rubles worth of supplemental aid that included cotton fabrics, clothing, pharmaceuticals, etc.; Hungary with 59 million rubles, plus 15 million rubles of supplemental aid; Bulgaria with 37 million rubles, plus 30 million rubles worth of foodstuffs, soap, cotton fabrics, clothing, shoes, pharmaceuticals, machinery, etc.; Albania with 9,000 tons of pitch, plus an additional 10,000 tons later; and Mongolia with 120,000 heads of livestock, 4,600 tons of foodstuffs, 30,000 sheep, 2,000 heads of cattle, and 5,000 tons of wheat.[27]

The level of Soviet influence was also reflected in terms of North Korea's reliance on Soviet models and Soviet experiences for their own programs of economic recovery.

A reliance on Chinese institutional patterns was not yet in the offing. It was to come later, at a more opportune time. However, by cutting in on the Soviet hegemony in Korea, a significant turnabout was brought about by the Chinese in Korea. The sudden interposition of the Chinese between Moscow and Pyongyang began to present Kim with increasing political latitude, and as he proceeded to gather the reins of power into his own hands, he also set in motion a trend that was eventually to place heavy strictures on Sino-Soviet influence in Pyongyang.

THE RISE OF KIM IL-SONG AND
THE DEATH OF STALIN

In 1945, when Kim Il-song first appeared on the national scene with obvious Russian support, he was in dire need of a viable self-image. But if an image of malleability cursed him as a Russian "puppet," it also earned him the acceptance of Stalin. Kim, according to one account, was acceptable to Stalin because he "had spent five or six years in the Soviet Union and his biography was transparent."[28]

The obstacles that confronted Kim were rooted in the existing political culture. In his first public appearance, it was alleged in unflattering terms that the Pyongyang citizenry, which was expecting a "gray-haired nationalist," was confronted by an obscure figure in his thirties who appeared wearing an ill-fitting blue suit, a haircut resembling a "Chinese waiter," and a dropping hairstyle that made him look like a "lightweight boxer."[29] If, as reported, Kim was met by a pronounced audience discomfiture it was because the ritual symbols of public form, that are as important as the substance of a ruler's thought, were ignored. Kim's sensitivity to that event necessitated revised accounts of his first public appearance.

> October 14, 1945 came at last! A Pyongyang City meeting was called to celebrate the triumphant return of Comrade Kim Il-song at the public playground. . . . Hearing that he was going to attend the meeting, the entire Pyongyang City seethed with excitement. This was the greatest joy ever to come to Pyongyang. . . . Comrade Kim Il-song appeared on the platform with an imposing and vigorous bearing and shouts of joy arose throughout the meeting place like a fiery wind and rousing cheers thundered. Crowds of people shouted "Long live General Kim Il-song!" dancing with joy and hugging each other. They looked like the broad expanse of sea at dawn, with its surf tinged golden with the rising sun.[30]

Moreover, the Pyongyang media is now compelled to publish only photographs of the occasion that show Kim standing alone on the speakers' platform. Other photographs taken on the occasion that depict Soviet officers standing behind Kim on the platform have been eliminated.[31]

Two basic assessments have emerged with respect to Kim Il-song's role during that period. First, there is the opinion that Kim was nothing but a puppet who responded willingly to Stalin's marching orders. There is also the contrary view that Kim was always an irrepressible nationalist who exercised far greater autonomy than he has been credited with in spite of the Russians and the Chinese.

However, the evidence also suggests that from 1945 to 1953 conditions changed that enabled Kim to move gradually from full reliance on the Soviet advisory group to increasing independence from both the Russians and the Chinese. Although the autonomy that Kim exercised in purging Soviet and Chinese-leaning rivals provides persuasive evidence of Kim's doggedness in that struggle, the independence that he exercised was by no means that of an irreverent helmsman infusing his own brand of Stalinism into the North Korean political culture. The unexpected upheavals visited on Korea by the war started the process of undercutting Soviet influence in Korea simply because Soviet directives did not always translate into Soviet controls in the trenches or in the hinterlands. When the CPV entered Korea, they diluted Soviet influence further with their mere presence.

On the Chinese side, it is unlikely that Peng Teh-huai was receptive to waging war in conjunction with a Korean leadership that was still amenable to Soviet "advice." When the Russian and Chinese preoccupation with themselves and with the war allowed Kim to move out increasingly on his own, Kim could very well have appeared as the source of the Sino-Soviet contradiction to Peng.

Much of Kim's success at that time can be attributed to the fact that his ruthlessness was not indiscriminate. Kim's actions were calculated. He carefully documented the charges leveled against his enemies and took his cases to the masses. He also used opposing factions to vie against each other for power to neutralize Sino-Soviet meddling in the internal affairs of Pyongyang. It was a matter of making everyone play the political game in Korea by Korean rules.

Until 1953, however, Soviet influence was greater than Chinese influence because of Soviet power and because of Stalin. It was Stalin who put Kim in power and it was Stalin to whom the North Koreans went for help in paying their bills and obtaining military assistance. Moreover, Stalin was both a mentor and model for Kim. Thus, when Stalin died, the Kremlin lost a source of influence that extended to the very pinnacle of power in the DPRK. Kim's link to Stalin was far too personal to be transferred to Khrushchev automatically. It was not the Korean way to Kim, who had become inured to the ways of personalized rule.

NOTES

1. Kim Il-song once remarked that, "All of the most precious and best things in the life of the Korean people are related to the name of Stalin. Stalin has become the flesh and blood of every Korean family living north of the thirty-eighth parallel and extending up to the Yalu River." Kim Il-song, Kim Il-song Sonjip (Collected Works of Kim Il-song), vol. 4 (Pyongyang: Korean Workers' Party Publishing House, 1953), p. 472.

2. Mao Tse-tung reportedly held out for four conditions prior to committing the CPV to Korea: (1) The commander of the joint headquarters and command staff would be headed by a Chinese and the deputy commander would be a Korean; (2) In both groups, the Chinese would have a majority and in case of a difference of opinion, the Chinese view would prevail; (3) There could be no agreement with any country on the matter of war or peace without the prior consent of the Chinese command; and (4) Chinese forces would not be subject to DPRK laws. Ch'oe Kyu-yon, Chunggong ui Kundae (The Chinese Communist Military) (Seoul: Songumsa, 1974), p. 159. It is unlikely that there were political demands to contravene Stalin's political controls in North Korea.

3. Kim Il-song's background is treated in Dae-Sook Suh, The Korean Communist Movement, 1918-1948 (Princeton: Princeton University Press, 1967), pp. 256-93; and Chong-Sik Lee, "Kim Il-song of North Korea," Asian Survey 7 (June 1967): 374-82.

4. Korean Central News Agency, Korean Central Yearbook, 1962, p. 207.

5. Ibid.

6. Wolfgang Leonhard, Child of the Revolution (Chicago: Henry Regnery Co., 1958), pp. 177-78.

7. The Kremlin's plans for the takeover of North Korea were apparently unknown to its allies. On July 13, 1945, while the treaty of neutrality was still in effect, the Japanese authorities asked the Soviet Union to act as an intermediary to bring the war to an end with the United States and Great Britain. The word was never passed on by the Kremlin and instead, the Soviet Union declared war on Japan less than a month later. Paul Hibbert Clyde, The Far East (New York: Prentice-Hall, 1952), p. 694.

8. Major works on the takeover of Korea include, U.S. Department of State, North Korea: A Case Study in the Techniques of Takeover, Department of State Publication No. 7118, Far Eastern Series No. 103 (Washington, D.C.: U.S. Government Printing Office, 1961), and Philip Rudolph, North Korea's Political and Economic Structure (New York: Institute of Pacific Relations, 1959). Other studies include, Kim Ch'ang-sun, Fifteen-Year History of

North Korea, U.S. Joint Publications Research Service, JPRS: 18,925 (April 26, 1963); and Robert A. Scalapino and Chong-Sik Lee, Communism in Korea (Berkeley: University of California Press, 1972).

9. Mark Gayn, "The Cult of Kim," New York Times Magazine, October 1, 1972, p. 28.

10. George F. Kennan, Memoirs: 1925-1950 (Boston: Atlantic Monthly Press, 1967), p. 395.

11. The inclination of Chinese statesmen to turn to Russia for assistance against the Japanese has long been rooted in history. Allen S. Whiting, China Crosses the Yalu: The Decision to Enter the Korean War (New York: Macmillan Co., 1960), p. 35.

12. The voting down of a Korean military assistance bill by the U.S. House of Representatives in January 1950 was a source of dismay in South Korea. Chum-Kon Kim, The Korean War (Seoul: Kwangmyong Publishing Co., 1973), p. 68.

13. Dean Acheson, Present at the Creation (New York: W. W. Norton, 1969), p. 357.

14. Khrushchev is alleged to have stated that, "I must stress that the war wasn't Stalin's idea but Kim Il-song's. Stalin of course didn't try to dissuade him. In my opinion, no real communist would have tried to dissuade Kim Il-song from his compelling desire to liberate South Korea from Syngman Rhee and from reactionary American influence. To have done so would have contradicted the Communist view of the world. I don't condemn Stalin for encouraging Kim. On the contrary I would have made the same decision myself if I had been in his place. Mao Tse-tung also answered affirmatively. He approved Kim Il-song's suggestion and put forward the opinion that the USA would not intervene since the war would be an internal matter which the Korean people would decide for themselves." Khrushchev Remembers, trans. and ed. by Strobe Talbott (Boston: Little Brown and Co., 1970), p. 368.

15. Harold C. Hinton, China's Turbulent Quest: An Analysis of China's Foreign Relations Since 1945 (New York: Macmillan, 1970), p. 42.

16. Richard C. Thornton, China, The Struggle for Power, 1917-1972 (Bloomington: Indiana University Press, 1973), p. 221.

17. For an analysis of Chinese motivations that led to the intervention see Whiting, op. cit.

18. Hinton, op. cit., p. 43.

19. In seeming fatalism, Mao once remarked that, "He who first made clay human idols to bury with the dead should have no posterity. I have no posterity, one son was killed in battle [in Korea] and another became mad." The source notes that, "This is a saying of Confucius, indicating his disapproval of the notion of human

sacrifice symbolized by the clay idols being buried with the dead. The saying later developed a broader meaning. He who initiates something evil will be severely punished by God." The Case of Peng Teh-huai, 1959-1968 (Hong Kong: Union Research Institute, 1968), p. 25.

20. According to a former Polish military attache, the Chinese kept all foreigners, including the Russians, away from the Chinese units in Korea. On one occasion, after much badgering by the Russians, the Chinese allowed a group of Soviet officers to visit a CPV unit. They were taken on a harrowing all-night drive "over mountains, rivers, and dark back roads" before reaching their quarters in a deep cave. For a week, they were mostly confined to their cave "for their own protection." They were consulted only once about a minor problem, which "any experienced Major could have figured out." "After another week of boredom and claustrophobia, the Russians suggested that they might as well go home. The Chinese quickly agreed, packed their guests into vehicles and got them back to the border. This time, the all-night trip took exactly one hour." Pawel Monat, "Russians in Korea: The Hidden Bosses," Life, June 27, 1960, p. 96.

21. Ibid., p. 77.

22. The Case of Peng, pp. 196-97.

23. The Research Institute of History, The Academy of Sciences of the DPRK, History of the Just Fatherland Liberation War of the Korean People (Pyongyang: Foreign Languages Publishing House, 1961).

24. Nodong Sinmun, September 7, 1964.

25. Pak Tong-un, "Communist China's Impact on North Korea," Seoul, Asea Yongu (The Journal of Asiatic Studies) 9, no. 3 (September 1966): 81.

26. Nodong Sinmun, September 8, 1968.

27. Pang Ho-sik, Sahoejuui Chinyong Naradul Kan ui Kisul Kyongjejok Hyopjo (Technical and Economic Cooperation Between the Countries of the Socialist Camp) (Pyongyang: Korean Workers' Party Publishing House, 1958), pp. 32-33.

28. Gayn, op. cit.

29. O Yong-chin, Hana Ui Chongon (An Eyewitness Account) (Pusan: Kungmin Sasang Chidowon, 1952), pp. 141-42.

30. Baik Bong, Kim Il-song Biography II (Tokyo: Miraisha, 1970), pp. 52-53.

31. See the first two photo plates in Scalapino and Lee, Communism in Korea, op. cit., vol. I.

CHAPTER 4

RECONSTRUCTION AND THE PROBLEM OF KHRUSHCHEV: 1954-64

The postwar reconstruction of the DPRK was directed toward the achievement of three goals: to place the country back on the tracks of Communist construction, to make the country increasingly impervious to outside influence through national self-strengthening, and to make the Communist North a more viable alternative to the democratic South. In order to achieve those goals, the consolidation of national power was deemed to be an overriding priority in Pyongyang.

The order of priorities were: a renewed commitment to national cohesiveness centered on Kim Il-song; modern industrialization centered mainly on heavy industry; and a well-ordered program of diplomacy centered on a balanced relationship with Moscow and Peking. The instruments of policy that Pyongyang chose to apply to those tasks included the purge in politics, mass-line techniques in economics, and the manipulation of Sino-Soviet differences in diplomacy.

Pyongyang's policy assumptions were sound. However, the death of Stalin suddenly eroded the conditions that supported those assumptions. The personal influence of Stalin on Kim Il-song ended as the struggle for power began in the Kremlin. Soviet entry into the policy councils of Pyongyang was abruptly closed off to the Kremlin and it suddenly ended the need in Pyongyang to rely on policy manipulation as an instrument of accommodation with Soviet interests. Behind closed doors, a concern for power replaced a concern for policy vis-a-vis the Kremlin. Kim's political survival was no longer tied to an evolution of values that included outside constraints as well as outside support. Once his rivals were out of the way, Kim was ready to force his own values on the North Korean political culture. By the time Khrushchev was in power and ready to exercise a renewed influence in Korea, conditions were already vastly altered in Pyongyang. Therein began the problem of Khrushchev.

THE RECONSTRUCTION PERIOD

The period ranging from 1953 to 1957 was called "the period to build the bases of socialism" in North Korea. It was a period devoted to the rehabilitation of the devastated DPRK economy. Most of North Korea's plants and installations were destroyed and the damage to the rural farming areas was also quite extensive.[1] However, the widespread devastation probably contributed to the success of the agricultural cooperatization movement carried out in North Korea during the period by disrupting the social patterns that sustained the deep-rooted conservatism in the countryside.

The experimental stage of agricultural collectivization was conducted between August and October 1954. A full-scale movement got underway in December 1954, and by August 1958 the task was completed in the country. However, in October 1958, just two months later, a fascination with the Chinese communes and a growing support for the Chinese line compelled the North Koreans to organize their cooperatives into larger units. The relevance of Maoist prescriptions to Pyongyang's quest for national reconstruction and the need to support a specifically Asian line against Khrushchev gradually became evident in Pyongyang.

North Korea's quest for independence was abetted during the period by Mao's increasing preoccupation with China's burgeoning domestic problems. China's point of departure from Soviet policies began in late 1957 and became progressively pronounced in early 1958 when Mao's righteous revolutionary attitude became the touchstone of China's voluntarist approach to revolutionary transformation. For Mao and Kim, the transformation of man became the key to the transformation of society. However, the revolutionary image tended to belie the highly practical considerations underlying the programs in Peking and Pyongyang. By the mid-1950s, both Mao and Kim had become sufficiently disenchanted with Soviet policy under Khrushchev to seek their own solutions to the problems of national self-strengthening. By force of circumstance, both leaders were forced to rely on their own resources and their own sources of tradition for inspirational guidance. Mao turned to the spirit of Yenan, while Kim sought to draw on the tradition of the Korean anti-Japanese struggle.[2]

The Chinese resolve to go it alone and adopt a policy of self-reliance struck a responsive chord in North Korea. The North Koreans concurred that: "Economic independence is the basis of political independence. Economic reliance on foreign forces entails political reliance on those forces. Economic subordination then leads to political subordination."[3]

The economic dividends of agricultural collectivization, which predated the Chinese effort but which was later influenced by Chinese models, included a rapid rehabilitation of the rural economy, a planned economic approach to the solution of an acute food shortage and a mechanism for the reallocation of workers at a time when the country was saddled with labor shortages.

However, by the time the final elements of the Chinese People's Volunteers had departed from the DPRK in 1958, significant changes had taken place to cause Kim to modify his attitudes toward China. The obvious North Korean experimentation with Chinese models tended to cloak fundamental transformations in the political order.

From 1945 to 1947, the Soviet occupation command created an administrative system that linked all local people's committees to its command center. The setup was used to control all major decisions and personnel assignments affecting North Korea. From a strictly utilitarian viewpoint, the policy was correct because it had been demonstrated during the Kabo Reforms of the 1890s that only a powerful leading force would be capable of implanting modern values in Korea.[4] By the end of the war, Kim was ready to usurp the functions instituted by the Soviet command with the aid of the Party apparatus. The political purges conducted by Kim Il-song through 1958 seem to indicate that in the postwar era, Kim was intent on creating a party-government bureaucracy that depended on loyalty to himself as the source of stability and cohesion. In the latter case, however, the watchdog functions formerly performed by strategically placed Soviet "advisers" were performed by his own loyal followers. By doing so, Kim was able to turn pro-Soviet and pro-Chinese figures in Pyongyang who were under suspicion into veritable puppets under his watchful eye. All dissidents rooted out under the system eventually succumbed to Kim's purges.[5] Kim's call for all "cadres and members of the Party" to "sharpen their vigilance against the activities of the factionalists" was particularly urgent during that period. Said he:

> . . . [T]he revolutionaries in our Party are composed of those from the Soviet Union, China, and various other places, as well as those who carried on struggles within the country, and those who came from South Korea after the liberation. Factionalists often try to use this situation for their own purposes.
> Among those who came from South Korea are persons who profess to be representatives of the people from South Korea. As soon as they rise to high positions, they behave as if they alone have

> found jobs for the people from South Korea and
> have the authority to use them as cat's-paws in
> their personal maneuvers. Li Sung Yop once en-
> ticed some comrades from South Korea in this way.
>
> Of the people from the Soviet Union, we can
> take Ho Ka-i as a typical example. He behaved as
> if he were the representative of those who came
> from the Soviet Union.
>
> As for the people from China, we can cite Pak
> Il-u. He considers himself their representative.
> Alleging that "Comrades from China are not pro-
> moted to leading posts" or that "People from the
> Soviet Union have different manners and customs
> than those who are from China," he stealthily
> schemed to gather around him comrades whose
> level of consciousness is low. [6]

In contrast to the "rectification campaign" waged in China between 1957 and 1958 in response to the disturbing examples of "internal contradictions" offered by the Hungarian and Poznan uprisings of 1956, Kim Il-song's response to the internal threat was swift retribution. Kim's personal campaign bore little resemblance to the methods of persuasion and "remolding" attempted in China.[7] In fact, Kim seemed to have taken advantage of China's domestic preoccupation to purge the pro-Chinese elements in Pyongyang in 1956 and 1958. Following that, Kim felt that a modicum of stability had been achieved. He claimed: "Never was there a time, throughout the history of the workers' and communist movement in our country, when our party was so consolidated organizationally and ideologically as it is today and when the whole party and all the people are so firmly united and rallied as one in ideology and will as they are today."[8]

However, by the Fourth Party Congress in 1961, the differences between Moscow and Peking were beginning to worry the leadership in Pyongyang. Pyongyang's instinctive reaction to the dispute was to remain neutral, but by then events were already conspiring to limit Pyongyang's options on the matter.

THE IMPACT OF THE CPSU TWENTIETH PARTY CONGRESS

The initial ripple that hinted of Sino-Soviet differences was evinced at the CPSU Twentieth Party Congress in February 1956. That the first ripple would turn into a maelstrom was an eventuality that could hardly stay the equanimity of the North Koreans who had come to see in their commitment to bloc unity a commitment to Korean redemption.

Pyongyang's instinctive choice in the Sino-Soviet dispute was neutralism with qualifications. Privately, it seemed to sympathize with the PRC since Khrushchev's "soft line" had the same geopolitical impact on Korea as it did on China. Kim's support of the Great Leap and the communes provided tacit indications of support. But in opting for neutralism they clearly hoped that the dispute would abate. Kim, after all, was indebted to both sides for survival and sustenance. Moreover, there is every reason to believe that Kim Il-song has always had a very high regard for the assistance rendered by both the Soviet Union and China. If Stalin's impact on Kim was paternal, Mao's impact was fraternal. However, the issues and circumstances forced Kim to make a choice between friendship and the DPRK national interest. It was a reluctant choice born of duress, and the conditions that led to a triggering of an intensely nationalistic and defensive response in Pyongyang were as much a product of Sino-Soviet proddings for support as they were of the so-called "imperialist" threat.

Pyongyang's initial response to the issues of the Soviet Twentieth Party Congress was a muted endorsement. Ch'oe Yong-kon, the North Korean delegate, expressed support for the Soviet program in his congratulatory speech to the Congress. The guarded response cloaked the private concerns of the North Korean leadership, which had yet to sort out the implications of Khrushchev's statements as preparations began in private to respond to calls for support from Moscow and Peking.[9]

In Pyongyang, the most explosive issue turned out to be Khrushchev's denigration of Stalin's personality cult. The political mood engendered by the climate of de-Stalinization prompted an attack on the emerging cult of Kim Il-song by Party dissidents in Pyongyang. Khrushchev's affront to the legend of Stalin was translated into a personal political affront to the ambitious North Korean ruler.

The coup attempted against Kim Il-song by Yong Kong-hum and Ch'oe Ch'ang-ik of the Yenan faction, and Pak Chang-ok of the Soviet faction, failed, and news of the incident triggered immediate reactions in Moscow and Peking. Anastas Mikoyan, who was reportedly in Peking when the events began to break, and Peng Teh-huai hurriedly flew into Pyongyang to mediate the Party leadership crisis. Peng and Mikoyan temporarily succeeded in smoothing over matters by attributing the incident to reasons common to parties in early stages of development.[10] Some of the conspirators were spared temporarily by the high-powered Sino-Soviet intervention but soon after most were charged with other crimes and speedily eliminated by Kim Il-song.

PROBLEM OF KHRUSHCHEV 53

The liberalization trend set in motion by Khrushchev was regarded by Kim to have had not only an untoward effect on Korea but also on China, where the Hundred Flowers Movement left Mao reeling from domestic dissidence.

Yet, although there is every reason to believe that the North Koreans harbored strong private misgivings about Khrushchev's policies, publicly there was nothing but public assent for Soviet policy. Neither the issues of "peaceful coexistence" nor the noninevitability of war occasioned any alarm in Pyongyang immediately following the Twentieth Party Congress. In summing up the developments of the late 1950s, Kim noted that:

> The Soviet Union and all other socialist states, proceeding from their consistent peaceful foreign policy, are striving to ensure the peaceful co-existence of nations with different social systems and to settle international disputes through negotiations. The proposals for disarmament and a series of other proposals put forward by the Soviet Union are of momentous significance in easing international tension and in preserving and consolidating peace. The Korean people fully support the sincere efforts and all the reasonable proposals by the Soviet Union which are aimed at curbing the imperialist policies of aggression and war and safeguarding world peace.[11]

As for the more sensitive issue of "collective leadership," Kim endorsed it as "the basis of Party committees' activities." There was no indication in writing or in practice that it meant anything to his personal leadership within the Party.

In the fall of 1961, to remain silent was to remain neutral and even though Kim was confident in stating that "the forces of socialism are decisively prevailing over the forces of imperialism," the depth of Kim's alarm over the military coup in South Korea that brought Pak Chong-hui to power was revealed in his hurry to conclude mutual security treaties first with Moscow, and then a week later with Peking, in July 1961. Kim Il-song still viewed Sino-Soviet unity as vital to North Korea's national interest even though he was aware that relations were on the downgrade between Moscow and Peking.

THE SINO-SOVIET RIFT: NEW DIMENSIONS IN THE NATIONAL INTEREST

Within a month after eulogizing the Soviet Union as "the hope of progressive mankind and the powerful bulwark of peace, national independence, and socialism," at the Fourth Congress of the KWP, Kim journeyed to Moscow to attend the Twenty-second Congress of the CPSU. The occasion marked Kim's personal exposure to the dimensions of the struggle between Moscow and Peking. Much to Kim's dismay, Khrushchev's denunciation of the Albanian Party as "dogmatist" occasioned a swift response from Chou En-lai, who regarded it to be "un-Marxist" to reveal "differences before the enemy and attack fraternal parties." In his address to the Congress, Kim himself refrained from criticizing either Stalinism or Albania.

There were indications of pressures brought to bear on Kim in Moscow on the issues of Stalin and Albania. Said Kim, in his report at the Second Plenum of the Fourth KWP Congress, "We recognize that no Party can interfere in the internal affairs of any of its fraternal Parties. This is one of the basic principles to which all fraternal Parties must adhere in their relations with each other. Therefore, the problem of Stalin and anti-Party factions in the Communist Party of the Soviet Union has nothing to do with our Party and cannot be a subject of discussion by or in our Party."[12] Two points were underscored in Kim's report. First, the need for bloc solidarity and second, the need to preserve the principles of independence and equality for each Party.

Throughout the period, however, the North Korean media continued to emphasize its continued recognition of the leading role played by the Soviet Union in bloc affairs. The overt publications indicated that from the first rumblings of the Sino-Soviet dispute to the end of 1962, Kim Il-song managed to remain neutral on the issues of the Sino-Soviet dispute. North Korean press releases reflected a policy of equal billing for both countries with complimentary statements presented with care to reflect a balanced treatment of both countries. At the same time, the press continued to push for an amelioration of relations between the two feuding powers.

However, a series of developments soon compelled Kim Il-song to lean more noticeably toward the Chinese side. The shift did not occur overnight. The shift was influenced by a combination of a transformation in the nature of the Sino-Soviet dispute and in the nature of the accompanying issues. Khrushchev's position on such matters as peaceful coexistence, on the idea of a peaceful transition to socialism, and the rhetoric of revisionism imputed to him by the Chinese side were essentially theoretical issues over which the ideologues from both sides sparred. Although the scholastic debates provided thinly veiled representations of more basic differences, the inclination to limit the debate to Party relations allowed the North Koreans, with their disinclination to involve themselves in messy ideological issues, to remain neutral. But as the acrimonious debate at the Party level led to a deterioration in state relations, the issues became increasingly infused with volatile potentialities for nationalistic conflicts between the two powers.

The grievances that the Chinese had accumulated until then were issues with which the North Koreans could very well have sympathized. They included Khrushchev's abrupt decision in 1959 to renege on an original promise to provide China with nuclear technology for building its own atomic bomb; Soviet support of India during its border clash with China in September 1959, compounded by resentments over the Soviet supply of arms to India during the Sino-Indian border clash of 1962; and the Soviet decision in 1960 to withdraw economic aid and technical assistance from China. Kim's resentment of the Soviet withdrawal of technical assistance was reflected in his well-known account of the difficulties encountered by Korean workers in trying to build a tractor without blueprints.[13]

Thus, when Sino-Soviet friction developed over the Sino-Indian border clash of 1962, the Cuban missile crisis, and Khrushchev's renewed courting of Tito, Kim Il-song sided with the Chinese. Moreover, both Peking and Pyongyang tended to view the threat posed by the U.S. military presence in Asia to their foremost foreign-policy objectives in the same light. The United States stood in the way of Peking's takeover of Taiwan just as it stood in the way of Pyongyang's occupation of South Korea. Both the Chinese and the North Koreans were therefore inclined to view the United States as a serious threat to both countries and both sides favored the adoption of a tough posture toward the United States rather than an attitude of conciliation. However, the Kremlin, which was faced with a tough Western stand on the German question, tended to regard the Chinese view of widespread bloodletting as a necessary risk as reeking too much of adventurism. North Korea's persistent support of China added to Khrushchev's discomfiture over the unacceptable risk of forcing a nuclear showdown with the United States, earning Pyongyang the displeasure of the Kremlin. Pyongyang's characterization of Soviet arms aid to India during the Sino-Indian border incident in the fall of 1962 as the work of "modern revisionists" acting as "servitors of imperialism" merely compounded Khrushchev's ire.[14]

Khrushchev's decision to back away from the brink during the Cuban missile crisis of 1962 also raised doubts in North Korea about Soviet commitments to the lesser countries of the bloc in any kind of confrontation with imperialism. There was a parallel between that backdown and the Kremlin's willingness to have let Korea go down the drain without the commitment of Soviet troops as conditions seemed to have dictated during the Korean War.

In December 1962 and January 1963, two further incidents compelled the North Koreans to side with the Chinese. At the Twelfth Congress of the Czechoslovakian Communist Party held in December

1962, the North Korean delegation was made an open target of rebuke by the pro-Soviet representatives in attendance when its spokesman attempted to protest against "continuing criticisms" against the Chinese. Also, at the Sixth Congress of the German Socialist Party held in January 1963, the head of the DPRK delegation was denied the privilege of delivering his speech to the gathering. Instead, only an abridged version of his speech was circulated among the delegates in attendance. The deliberate snub drew an editorial criticism from the North Korean Party organ.

> All fraternal parties are independent and equal and shape their policies independently in keeping with the principles of Marxism-Leninism and proceeding from the specific conditions of their countries. There are big countries and small countries, but there is no high party and low party. Precisely for this reason, no party should interfere in the internal affairs of other fraternal parties or exert pressures on them, force their unilateral will upon them and slander them.[15]

Beginning in January 1963, therefore, North Korea began to support China far more openly on bloc issues. By that time, there was also a convergence of Chinese and Korean views on the question of revisionism. Initially, the North Koreans, unlike the Chinese, had been careful to refer to the "revisionists" as "the modern revisionists, represented by the Tito clique in Yugoslavia." The purpose then had been to avoid direct criticism of the Soviet Union. As relations with Moscow worsened, the inclination to use the surrogate term was dropped and in November 1962, as Tito himself prepared to journey to Moscow on a fence-mending mission, the North Korean media bitterly complained that, "While making all-out efforts to distort the principles of Marxism-Leninism to deprive it of revolutionary spirit, modern revisionists, as ideological hirelings of U.S. imperialism, are unhesitatingly pursuing, at the imperialists' instigation, their vicious policy of slandering and dividing the socialist countries in an attempt to overthrow the parties and governments of these countries."[16]

It is difficult to say whether the North Koreans were more emboldened or incensed by the developments surrounding the dispute. Nevertheless, they pressed their attack on Khrushchev by criticizing the idea that the USSR had been transformed from a proletarian dictatorship into a "state of the whole people," as stated in the new Party program that was adopted under Khrushchev at the Twenty-second Party Congress.

> . . . The modern revisionsists state that from the time that the socialist production relations became wholly predominant, the socialist state is not an organ of the proletarian dictatorship but changes to a classless organ and the dictatorship of the proletariat is no longer required once it enters the period of communist construction.[17]

The North Korean view was that such a stand would lead to an abandonment of the class struggle and a surrender to "counterrevolutionary economism" under conditions prevailing in countries like Korea. The depth of the North Korean commitment was expressed in the commentary that, ". . . the political struggle of the working class, including armed struggle, is the highest form of class struggle. Because the question of the dictatorship of the proletariat too, is a question of power, it is the sharpest question of principle on which a Marxist-Leninist can make no concession whatsoever."[18]

THE MANAGEMENT OF PRESSURES FROM THE CHINESE

As the Sino-Soviet dispute grew in intensity, the PRC undertook a diplomatic campaign to enlist the support of the Asian Communist parties. In April and May 1963, PRC Chairman Liu Shao-ch'i paid an unprecedented visit to four Southeast Asian countries.

Following that, an exchange of state visits was arranged between the People's Republic of China and the Democratic People's Republic of Korea. There was room for speculation that the Chinese initiative was calculated to bring about a final settlement of views between Peking and Pyongyang.

The significance of the Sino-Korean exchange of state visits was heightened by the fact that the DPRK state visit to China was to occur just a month prior to the opening of the Sino-Soviet discussions (on July 5, 1963 in Moscow) on ways to reconcile the differences between the two countries. Liu Shao-ch'i's visit to the DPRK was to follow in September 1963.

On June 5, 1963, Ch'oe Yong-kon, North Korea's titular counterpart to Liu Shao-ch'i, journeyed to Peking to begin his state visit. On that day, the <u>Nodong Sinmun</u>, the North Korean Party newspaper, printed an editorial to mark the event. The editorial paid tribute to the assistance rendered by the Chinese during the Korean War. It upheld the contention that nations must find and develop their own paths to communism in endorsing the concept of self-reliance and it went on to deliver a vitriolic condemnation of U.S. imperialism. However, hardly a word was said about the crucial theoretical issues of the bloc.

On the other hand, the Chinese <u>Jen-min Jih-pao</u> that appeared on the same day inferred that North Korea was on its side in noting the "irreconcilable struggle" of the Korean Workers' Party against "modern revisionism." Throughout his visit, however, Ch'oe Yong-kon showed himself to be quite circumspect on the issue of revisionism.

In other words, there was no final settlement in the offing and the North Koreans remained firm in their determination not to be pressured by the Chinese into taking an unequivocal stand against Khrushchev or the CPSU. In the long joint statement that was released at the conclusion of the state visit, it was merely agreed that "the Tito clique of Yugoslavia is typical of modern revisionism."[19]

On September 8, 1963, just prior to the Liu Shao-ch'i state visit to North Korea, a celebration was held in Pyongyang to mark the fifteenth anniversary of the establishment of the DPRK. Ch'oe Yong-kon delivered a major speech on that occasion in which he fully ignored the role played by the Soviet Union in establishing the DPRK. Instead, he emphasized that the republic was "founded by the [Korean] people themselves." At the same time, in a further display of independence, he made no mention of the Chinese contribution to the DPRK during the Korean War. Ch'oe emphasized instead that, "In the three years of the fierce fatherland liberation war, the Korean people repulsed the armed invasion of U.S. imperialism and its puppets and defended with their lives the independence and honor of the Democratic People's Republic of Korea."[20] The North Koreans made it amply clear that the principle of independence applied to all powers, including the Chinese, and also communicated to the Kremlin that if there was a disagreement, it was a Korean disagreement and not a disagreement that was calculated merely to support the Chinese stand against the Soviet Union. As far as the Koreans were concerned, there was a principle involved that, by implication, also left the door open for a future improvement in relations once the substantive issues were settled.

On September 15, 1963, Liu Shao-ch'i arrived in Pyongyang to begin his state visit. Again, there were noticeable efforts by Liu to claim North Korean support for China's campaign against Khrushchev. The North Korean response was guarded.[21] Instead of joining with China to criticize the Soviet Union on the substantive issues of the bloc, the North Korean side chose instead to criticize the Kremlin about the "errors" on Korean history contained in a Korean history book compiled by the USSR Academy of Sciences.[22] The strain in Korean-Chinese relations was evident at the end of Liu's state visit.

Unlike the long joint statement released at the conclusion of Ch'oe Yong-kon's state visit to Peking, Liu Shao-ch'i's state visit to North Korea ended with the release of a terse and perfunctory "press communique."[23]

Meanwhile, two highly significant events had taken place between Ch'oe Yong-kon's visit to the PRC and Liu Shao-ch'i's return visit to the DPRK. First, it was quite obvious that the Chinese and Soviet delegations had reached an impasse in their attempts to bring about a reconciliation between the two sides in Moscow. Among the officials accompanying Liu Shao-ch'i to Pyongyang was Wu Hsiu-chuan, who had also gone to Moscow as a member of the Chinese delegation to the Sino-Soviet talks. Wu Hsiu-chuan's presence at the side of Liu in Pyongyang at a time of heightened intensity in the Sino-Soviet polemic meant that the key issues of the Sino-Soviet dispute and China's stand with respect to those issues were aired at the Sino-Korean talks in Pyongyang.

It should also be noted that on July 25, 1963, the Soviet Union became a signatory to the Limited Nuclear Test Ban Treaty at the very time that the PRC delegation, led by Teng Hsiao-ping, was in Moscow exploring ways to effect a Sino-Soviet reconciliation. The Chinese view of the event as final proof that the Soviet leadership had begun to collude with "U.S. imperialism" to shackle China and the scathing terms with which it chose to denounce the Soviet Union, worsened relations between the two countries even further. Yet, the press communique that was released at the end of Liu's visit to the DPRK failed to touch on either of those issues.

In spite of the effusive exchange of compliments and the overt displays of unity manifested publicly by both sides during Liu Shao-ch'i's visit to North Korea, there was no indication of an unqualified North Korean commitment to the Chinese line. In fact, the North Koreans waited a full month prior to releasing a statement on the issues raised during Liu's visit. The North Korean media openly criticized and deplored the efforts of the "modern revisionists" to isolate China and the "practice of one side interfering in the other's internal affairs and demanding unilateral respect."

It was obvious from the events of that period that while the North Koreans admired the Chinese for their pluck and their Socialist innovations, their main strategy was still to steer a neutral course between the two feuding powers. But when the press of circumstances made it impossible to remain neutral, Kim Il-song chose to lean toward Mao rather than Khrushchev. Yet, Mao's stand on the practical issues of the bloc only provided pragmatic solutions to the problems of political, military, and economic underdevelopment. The Chinese stand on any issue reflected the Chinese view of themselves and not of the Koreans. Thus, as much as Chinese policy was capable of

commanding positive assent in Pyongyang, it could not convey a
Korean sense of identity or purpose. Without that, there was to be
no identity of purpose between Pyongyang and any other power. In
the source of the Chinese despair over Pyongyang's reluctance to be
a pawn was to be seen the ire of the Soviet leadership over Korean
intransigence.[24]

THE FALL OF KHRUSHCHEV: THE END OF AN ERA

Kim Il-song's earlier reluctance to disagree publicly with
Khrushchev may have included private grievances. However, the
issues that openly divided the two leaders were more obvious.

Khrushchev's desire to avoid risking nuclear war with the
United States, though understandable to the North Koreans, probably
became overly restrictive to the DPRK at the point when it began
to restrict North Korean initiatives for Korean unification. The inordinate concern for the Soviet national interest at the expense of
the North Korean national interest was bound to be resented at some
point.

Khrushchev's regard for peaceful coexistence as a principal
cornerstone of Soviet policy clashed with Kim Il-song's national developmental and defense interests. While there were ideological
issues at stake, the practical issue was that a Soviet hard line vis-
a-vis the West, over which the Sino-Soviet rift first developed, was
more in keeping with Kim's interest. Khrushchev's quest was regarded by Kim as unprincipled and born of a phobia of war. From
Kim Il-song's standpoint, peaceful coexistence offered a poor alternative to other more militant options for Korean unification.

Khrushchev's assertion that the role of the Communist Party
under a "state of the whole people" was to serve all of the people
rather than a specific class disturbed the North Koreans, who tended
to see capitalism lurking just beyond the thirty-eighth parallel in the
form of the U.S. presence in the South and in Japan. Pyongyang's
fear of cultural infiltration was just as acute as its fear for the
DPRK's national security. As far as Kim was concerned, a proletarian dictatorship was imperative as long as he was faced by "class
enemies" at home and abroad.

However, throughout the period of strained relations between
Moscow and Pyongyang, Soviet-Korean communications were apparently kept firmly intact. Throughout the intense debate between
Moscow and Peking, even though the North Koreans joined in directing harsh comments against Soviet policy, the Kremlin refrained
from retaliating with recriminatory attacks against Pyongyang. It
is conceivable that throughout that complex era, private communica-

tions between Moscow and Pyongyang remained intact in spite of the overt signs of coolness and that each side was kept apprised of the mood and moves of the other.

Kim Il-song's attitude toward Khrushchev was influenced considerably by China's independent stand in the Sino-Soviet dispute. However, by the time the CPV departed from Korea in 1958, significant changes had already taken place to influence Kim's attitude toward the Chinese. By then, because of the political purges of 1956 and 1958, Kim was firmly in control of the internal instruments of power and his growing independence began to be reflected in acts such as the curtailment of the use of Chinese characters in North Korea soon after the departure of the CPV.[25]

Developments within China itself had also begun to erode Mao's influence in Korea. When the Hundred Flowers campaign backfired on Mao, adding to reminders of earlier problems with liberalization in East Europe, it became clear to Kim Il-song that a tough organizational approach to Socialist construction would still be required in North Korea.

Moreover, the "flying horse movement" in North Korea was meeting with relative success at a time when its counterpart and inspiration, the Chinese Great Leap Forward, was foundering. Unlike China, the North Koreans stopped short of pushing the masses to utter limits of exhaustion. Moreover, inasmuch as the North Korean economy was basically an industrial economy already, the economy in general was not as vulnerable to agricultural failures as China was.[26] In China, poor harvests brought on by droughts, floods, and manpower imbalances dealt severe blows that were quickly transmitted throughout the economy.

Being a smaller country, the North Koreans were also able to apply economic controls far more expeditiously than the Chinese. The North Koreans were also in a far better position to benefit from Soviet advice and assistance while the excesses of the Great Leap Forward were being frowned upon by the Kremlin. The North Koreans emerged from that period with ideas of their own on economic management. While the Chinese models were valuable, they had to be tailored to Korean requirements.

In the early 1960s, to goad the masses into Socialist construction the braking effect of old ideas had to be eliminated. The narrowness of time-honored loyalties to the family, the village, and to traditional Korean ways had to be replaced by a more pervasive sense of loyalty to extrafamilial collectivities, to national priorities, and to the requirements of modernization. To the young North Korean regime, the only way was to seek a "conscious" form of national involvement by the people through ideological indoctrination and active political participation. The place of work became the starting point for participatory involvement and "collective leadership."

> Collective leadership requires that the wisdom
> and strength of many comrades be pooled. This
> necessitates that all learn from and teach each
> other, and help each other in a comradely way.
> When a comrade puts forward a certain view, has
> he not some grounds for it however insignificant
> it may seem? Hence his view must not be turned
> down pointblank but must be studied carefully,
> and efforts should be made to pick out its rational
> kernel, even if the view is not a hundred per cent
> correct. Only when everyone takes such an atti-
> tude towards others, can the opinions of the Party
> committee members be readily coordinated into
> well refined collective views, and a Party com-
> mittee function actively as a united organ of col-
> lective leadership.[27]

Obviously, the North Korean conception of "collective leadership" had little to do with the collective leadership that Khrushchev had in mind. The North Koreans had simply applauded Khrushchev for what they thought the concept should mean to themselves.

The political efficacy of the mass line was quite obvious to Kim Il-song from the outset. Aside from mobilizing initiative for economic purposes, it provided Kim with political controls all the way down to the village level. Once the system was in operation, Kim was ready for the tasks of further political consolidation and economic development. It also meant that at that point the country was that much more immune to outside tampering.

Increased power at home gave Kim greater flexibility to deal with Moscow and Peking. Ultimately, the flexibility served Kim well. In October 1964, Nikita Khrushchev fell from power, thereby removing the prime obstacle to the normalization of Korean-Soviet relations. Kim stood ready to exploit the new opening to Moscow.

NOTES

1. According to North Korea, most of the plants turning out ores, pig iron, steel, copper, lead, coke, ammonium sulphate fertilizer, carbide, caustic soda, cement, etc., were completly destroyed. "National Economic Development in the DPRK, 1945-1950" (Pyongyang: Foreign Languages Publishing House, 1960), p. 14.

2. For diplomatic reasons, Chinese sources have carefully avoided mentioning the fact that Kim was under the control of the Chinese Communist Party (CCP) during that period. They have even

more studiously avoided mentioning Korean vassalage under Chinese suzerainty. Pak Tong-un, "Communist China's Impact on North Korea," Seoul, Asea Yongu 9, no. 3 (September 1966): 53.

3. Nodong Sinmun, April 11, 1963.

4. A Korean scholar notes that, "Conditions in Korea at that time had not yet matured to the point where these [modern] values could develop themselves and a strong class capable of standing in the vanguard and supporting these values could not be formed. Thus, the values in Korea were not formed in response to the growth of objective conditions within the country, but were brought in from outside by some intellectuals and reformers who belonged to the upper stratum, or were demanded by foreign powers. Generally speaking, they were not original values that were rooted in and sprung from the realities of Korean life." Yi Man-kap, "Hanguk Sahoe ui Kach'i Kujo" (The Value Structure of Korean Society), Seoul, Sasanggye (May 1961): p. 67.

5. An examination of the major figures purged between 1952 and 1960 reveals that they were people who functioned at all levels of the Party and government bureaucracies. U.S. Joint Publications Research Service, Translations on North Korea, "Biographical Data on 492 Prominent North Koreans," no. 42, JPRS: 40,950 (May 9, 1967).

6. Kim Il-song, Selected Works, vol. 1 (Pyongyang: Foreign Languages Publishing House, 1965), pp. 297-98.

7. Pak Tong-un, op. cit., p. 64.

8. Kim Il-song, Selected Works, op. cit., vol. 2, p. 227.

9. One of the first signs of the public awareness of Stalin's fall from grace came in a Nodong Sinmun reprint of a Pravda editorial entitled, "Why is the Cult of the Individual Alien to Marxism-Leninism?" on April 2, 1956. Also, the Soviet representative to the Third Congress of the KWP held in April 1956 was Leonid Brezhnev, who addressed himself to the "Marxist-Leninist propositions" set forth at the Twentieth Party Congress in Pyongyang, Third Congress of the Workers' Party of Korea: Documents and Materials (Pyongyang: Foreign Languages Publishing House, 1956), p. 424.

10. Kim Ch'ang-sun, Fifteen-Year History of North Korea, U.S. Joint Publications Research Service, JPRS: 18,925 (April 26, 1963), pp. 102-04.

11. Kim Il-song, Selected Works, op. cit., vol. 2, pp. 266-67.

12. Nodong Sinmun, November 28, 1961.

13. "The hardest nut to crack in the production of a tractor was that we did not have a single sheet of blueprint. We took a tractor apart, worked out a design for each of its accessories and started cutting the accessories according to the designs. . . . When making the back wheel of the tractors, we collected steel sheets, welded

them together and hammered the crooked parts after heating them in the oxyacetylene flame and thus beat them into shape, instead of making them by the pressing and forging method. As regards the reflector case which is ordinarily made of soft steel sheets formed by the pressing method, we made it by beating metals into shape. We suffered failures 36 times before we finally succeeded in manufacturing it. It is, therefore, not necessary to recount here the stories of how we made the oil pressure apparatus whose manufacture requires delicate technical skills. Our hearts throbbed when we, having assembled the tractor, tested the operation of the engine. But for some unknown reason, the engine would not work. After a week's painstaking effort, we put in order what was wrong with the oil pressure apparatus and again started the engine. This time the engine worked. We thrust the gear lever in 'Forward' and stepped hard on the accelerator. The tractor, however, moved backward, not forward. The engine stopped working. . . . We overhauled the tractor and looked into what was wrong, but there was no way for us to find out which accessory was missing because we lacked accurate blueprints. . . . To our regret, such blueprints were not available to us." Kim Gum San, "In the Revolutionary Spirit of Self-Reliance," Democratic People's Republic of Korea (Pictorial), no. 137, 1967, pp. 4-7.

14. Nodong Sinmun, November 17, 1962.
15. Nodong Sinmun, January 30, 1963.
16. Nodong Sinmun, November 17, 1962.
17. "The Class Nature of the State," Kulloja, no. 19 (October 1963), trans. in U.S. Joint Publications Research Service, Translations of Political and Sociological Information on North Korea, no. 54, JPRS: 23,876 (March 26, 1964), pp. 1-6.
18. Byong-Sik Kim, Modern Korea: The Socialist North, Revolutionary Perspectives in the South (New York: International Publishers, 1970), p. 21.
19. Korean Central News Agency broadcast, June 24, 1963.
20. Nodong Sinmun, September 9, 1963.
21. Ch'oe's reticence was not a reflection of North Korea's approval of "modern revisionism." In late July, the Party theoretical journal carried the statement that, "certain people hold that the liberation of people who are weaker can be brought about through negotiations with the enemy. In other words, they hold that in the national liberation struggle, problems can be solved by sending a few representatives of the dependent countries to their metropolitan overlords to beg them for a change of heart instead of through a struggle of the masses." The North Korean objection to revisionism was intact but they were determined to speak out on their own rather than relying on the Chinese to do it for them. See, Kulloja, no. 14 (July 20, 1963): p. 24.

22. Kim Sok-hyung, Kim Hu-il, and Son Yung-chong, <u>On the Grave Errors in the Descriptions of Korea of the "World History" Edited by the USSR Academy of Sciences</u> (Pyongyang: Foreign Languages Publishing House, 1963).

23. <u>Nodong Sinmun</u>, September 27, 1963.

24. A Japanese observer noted that during a DPRK celebration on September 8, 1963, Ch'oe Yong-kon's report was greeted with thunderous applause but the Soviet Ambassador and other Soviet representatives refused to clap and "looked on with indifference." Koichi Yamamoto, "My Interview with Kim Il-song," <u>Ekonomisto</u> (Economist) (November 5, 1963), trans. in <u>Summaries of Selected Japanese Magazines</u>, American Embassy, Tokyo, December 2, 1963, p. 14.

25. Since the early days of the DPRK, the North Korean mass media refrained from using Chinese characters (<u>hanja</u>) in their vernacular publications. They relied exclusively on their own writing system (<u>hangul</u>). The order in 1958 probably went farther, suggesting reforms extending to root-word derivations. Kim once remarked that, "There is no need to use Chinese characters. The Chinese themselves who created the Chinese characters find them difficult to learn and cumbersome to use and are thinking of discarding them sometime in the future so why should we use them?" Kim Il-song, <u>Kim Il-song Chojak Sonjip</u> (Selected Writings of Kim Il-song), vol. 4 (Pyongyang: Korean Workers' Party Publishing House, 1968), p. 9.

26. Joungwon A. Kim, "The Peak of Socialism in North Korea: The Five and Seven-Year Plans," <u>Asian Survey</u> 5, no. 5 (May 1965): 261.

27. Kim Il-song, <u>Selected Works</u>, op. cit., vol. 2, pp. 264-65.

CHAPTER 5

THE PERILS OF INDEPENDENCE AND BELLIGERENCY: 1965-69

In the late 1960s, North Korea's problem in thinking big was in being small. Once the dispute escalated between Moscow and Peking, like the proverbial Korean "shrimp" there was no escaping the backlash of the "whales." If there was nothing redeeming in that condition, there was in the signboard of "independence" that was hoisted in Pyongyang. There was defiance in the mood of the North Koreans; a defiance that was soon to be joined by belligerency. For a country in despair over a dispute that it was powerless to control, there was relief in a belligerency that was to become the hallmark of North Korean policies during the latter part of the 1960s. Pyongyang's signboard reflected two fundamental concerns. First, the concern that the so-called "fraternal" countries were being needlessly coerced into taking sides in the Sino-Soviet dispute, and, second, the concern that the prolonged dispute was beginning to hurt the "anti-imperialist" and national revolutionary struggles of the small countries.

The belligerency that emerged out of Pyongyang served to dramatize the intense concern of the North Koreans and to provide a face-saving front to veil their dismay over the turn of events. Pyongyang's open militancy provided a bold front to cover the stresses caused by repeated rebuffs visited on it by Moscow and Peking, and served notice that any future initiatives for conciliation would have to come from Moscow or Peking. Pyongyang's concern for "face" was apparently understood by Soviet Premier Kosygin in February 1965 when he suddenly departed from a scheduled tour to fly into Pyongyang on what appeared to be a fence-mending mission.

THE IMPLICATIONS OF THE KOSYGIN
VISIT TO PYONGYANG

The Kosygin visit to Pyongyang was preceded by a number of significant developments. On January 8, 1965, just about a month prior to Kosygin's surprise visit to Pyongyang, South Korea dispatched a contingent of 2,000 troops to South Vietnam in a highly symbolic gesture of support for the Saigon government's anti-Communist struggle. Moreover, on February 7, 1965, even with the announced presence of Premier Kosygin and his party in Hanoi, President Lyndon Johnson ordered air strikes on North Vietnamese military targets. By February 25, 1965, South Korea had also moved to send a 600-man engineering unit to South Vietnam.[1]

Moreover, almost immediately after the fall of Khrushchev, a change of attitude quickly emerged in the North Korean media. The harsh DPRK attitude toward the Soviet Union was immediately replaced by a wait-and-see attitude. Kim Il-song obviously expected the cue to come from the Kremlin. The cue came with the Kosygin visit to Pyongyang.

The Kosygin visit elicited heavy play from the North Korean press. There was none of the "chill" that had reportedly marked Kosygin's reception in Peking shortly before that. During his visit, Kosygin quickly emphasized that his purpose was to seek to strengthen the relationship between the two countries through "an exchange of opinions on the question of the international situation and other problems of concern to our Parties and our countries."[2] Although Kosygin had arrived in Pyongyang as the Soviet government representative, it was clear that his discussions would range beyond state matters to party affairs. He blamed "imperialist intrigues" as the cause of dissension within the international Communist movement and emphasized the need to develop and strengthen "fraternal friendship" between the peoples of the Soviet Union and Korea and between their "militant parties." In turn, Kim Il-song stated that the meeting with the Soviet delegation promoted "mutual understanding" and served to strengthen the friendship between the peoples of the two countries. Further evidence of a transformation in relations came from the Kremlin in April, when Petr Demichev, head of the CPSU Ideological Commission, reported that the meeting in Pyongyang produced "a definite group of general political questions" on which the CPSU and the Korean Workers' Party "coincide or have come closer to each other."[3]

Soviet-Korean relations were exacerbated during Khrushchev's era when Party differences spilled over into state differences. The Kosygin visit, by restoring the distinction between party and state relations, allowed state relations between Moscow and Pyongyang to improve. Up until then, North Korea's military and economic development programs had been retarded by Moscow's decision to curtail Soviet military and economic assistance to the DPRK. The Soviet decision was in retribution for Pyongyang's decision to side with Peking on the ideological issues of the bloc. The immediate impact of the Soviet retribution was to disrupt the DPRK Seven-Year Economic Plan just as the ROK was embarking on its economic takeoff with U.S. and Japanese assistance, and as its dispatch of troops to South Vietnam was giving it increased international recognition.

Suddenly, Kim Il-song was confronted by a challenge from the South that only Moscow was capable of aiding. With the downfall of Khrushchev, who had punished Pyongyang for its intransigence, Kosygin's visit presented a welcome opening to the Kremlin for Kim Il-song since it would otherwise have been impossible for him to deal with a leader who had tried to cow him into submission. It also allowed Kosygin to determine whether the dispatch of more regular North Vietnamese units into South Vietnam would embolden Kim into launching his own march South.[4] The Soviet military and economic aid that soon followed into Pyongyang was probably predicated on a promise by Kim to at least maintain the status quo in the Korean peninsula.

In March, following the Kosygin visit, Kim continued to display his independence by refusing to attend a preparatory meeting of bloc parties called by the CPSU but at the same time, he tempered his attitude toward the Kremlin by suspending North Korean media references to "modern revisionism" as the main danger to the international Communist movement.

THE MOVE BACK TO THE MIDDLE

A shift in North Korea's policy line was in the offing but it was not articulated until April when Kim Il-song embarked on a rare trip abroad to Indonesia. During his visit, Kim delivered at the Aliarcham Academy of Social Sciences of Indonesia a major policy statement entitled, "On Socialist Construction in the Democratic People's Republic of Korea." There was nothing extraordinary in Kim's enumeration of the tasks, achievements, and hardships faced by the North Koreans during the protracted struggle to build socialism in the North and establish revolutionary conditions in the South. What was unprecedented was his frank and pointed discussion of the issues of the bloc and the relationship of those issues to the DPRK.

In essence, Kim's lecture centered on making chuche the cornerstone of North Korea's independent policy. Most significantly, his statement of independence was aimed mainly at Moscow and

PERILS OF INDEPENDENCE 69

Peking. In speaking out for Korean independence, he pulled no punches and he was particularly pointed in implicating Soviet efforts in the 1950s to intrude into the internal affairs of the DPRK.

> As is known, the years 1956-1957 were those when modern revisionism emerged on a wide scale in the international communist movement and availing themselves of this opportunity, the world imperialists and reactionaries unfolded an extensive anti-communist campaign, stepped up their reactionary offensive against the North on an unprecedented scale. At the same time the anti-Party revisionist elements within the Party came out to attack the Party, taking advantage of the complicated situation and banking on the support of outside forces. The anti-Party elements within the Party and their supporters abroad, revisionists--big power chauvinists, lined up as one in opposition to our Party and resorted to subversive activities in an attempt to overthrow the leadership of our Party and Government.[5]

In the economic realm, Kim drew a parallel between Japanese economic policy during the colonial era and Soviet economic policy during Khrushchev's era. Said Kim, "With the sole aim of plundering Korea of her resources and exploiting her people, the Japanese imperialists built in our country only a few branches of industry aimed at the production of raw materials and semi-finished goods."[6] Of the Soviet economic policy, Kim stated that, "The revisionists, talking about 'international division of labor' opposed our Party's line on the building of heavy industry and maintained, among other things, that our country did not need to develop the machine-building industry but would do well to produce only minerals and other raw materials."[7] Kim, of course, found that view completely unacceptable.

But the significant point of the lecture was not just the fact that the Soviet leadership or anyone else had intruded on the affairs of the North Koreans. An even more significant point made was that the North Koreans developed well in spite of their backwardness and the unwanted intrusions simply because they were able to rely on themselves and not on the Russians or the Chinese.

> While resolutely fighting in defense of the purity of Marxism-Leninism against revisionism, our Party has made every effort to establish chuche

> in opposition to dogmatism and flunkeyism.
> <u>Chuche</u> in ideology, independence in politics,
> self-reliance in economics and self-defense in
> national defense--this is the stand that our
> Party has consistently adhered to.[8]

Kim's statement of independence came in the aftermath of North Korea's support for China's ideological line and after a debilitating bout with the early rigors of economic self-reliance. It was, as Kim stated, also a period during which the "revisionists and big power chauvinists" attempted to overthrow Kim because of his Stalinist cult. Kim, it will be recalled, purged the "anti-Party elements" in 1956 and 1958, which led to the creation of the first Kim Il-song-dominated Political Committee at the Fourth Party Congress of 1961. The significance of the purges of 1956 and 1958, which was only alluded to in Kim's lecture, was that it involved the removal of pro-Chinese as well as pro-Soviet elements from the Korean Workers' Party. Therefore, in rejecting "dogmatism and flunkeyism" and opting for chuche, Kim clearly expected both Moscow and Peking to read his signals.

Kim's lecture in Indonesia, as a major statement of policy by a Communist Party leader on his first visit outside of the Communist bloc, was certain to have been monitored closely by the Soviet and Chinese Parties. Yet, neither the media of the Soviet Union nor China carried the lecture by Kim Il-song.

Kim's independent stand emerged amid the backdrop of significant domestic and foreign developments. By the end of 1963, North Korea was nearing the end of the first phase of its Seven-Year Plan, which was to be devoted to the stabilization of an economy that had been destabilized by the excesses of the "flying horse movement." The remedial measures adopted in Pyongyang included improvements in the mining and resource allocation sectors that were to allow the DPRK to go back to sustaining further heavy industrial development. From 1964 to 1967, plans called for a renewed commitment to the development of heavy industry with parallel developments in light industry and agriculture. By then, it had become quite obvious to Pyongyang that only Moscow was capable of providing the type of assistance that was required to accomplish those tasks. During the first phase of the Seven-Year Plan, the diversion of increasing national resources to national defense requirements and drastic cutbacks in Soviet aid had led to serious economic setbacks.[9] Kim's refusal to join the Soviet-dominated Council for Mutual Economic Assistance cost Pyongyang millions in economic assistance and in addition, it created an enormous disparity between its own limited levels of output and the levels of capitalization that foreign aid would have made possible for the purchase of foreign equipment and the related activity of establishing credit.

On the other hand, there was not much assistance forthcoming from China, which had been forced to temporarily forego heavy industry development emphasized under the Great Leap in favor of agricultural development.

The statement of independence made by Kim Il-song in Indonesia meant that while state relations would improve, Pyongyang still reserved the right to disagree with Moscow on the substantive issues of the bloc. An indication that North Korean independence had been raised to a new plateau soon became evident when, on the occasion of the anniversary observance of the Chinese People's Volunteers' entry into the Korean War, amid the usual window dressing of praise, the North Koreans editorially reminded the Chinese that their volunteers had after all come into Korea "to save the Chinese revolution," and, by implication, not the North Korean revolution.[10]

Although the economic factor was vital to the redevelopment of a preponderant Soviet influence in Pyongyang, by 1965 there were also pressing military issues that required a reassessment of relationships with Moscow. Pyongyang's support of Soviet policy was suddenly enhanced when the Kremlin reacted promptly and with vehemence to the first U.S. air strikes on North Vietnam in February 1965 by promising "to strengthen the defensive capability of the Democratic Republic of Vietnam" with arms shipments that would include surface-to-air missiles.[11]

North Korean apprehensions were stirred further with the signing of the ROK-Japan Treaty on June 22, 1965.[12] The Treaty was regarded in Pyongyang as having given South Korea the added benefit of support from a renascent Japanese nation along with U.S. support. The perceived threat in Pyongyang was probably serious enough to warrant going back under the Soviet nuclear umbrella as a contingency against the threat of an American attack on North Korea. It was hardly surprising, therefore, that North Korea agreed to accept Soviet aid to solve its critical oil supply problem in March 1965 as the Japanese-South Korean talks progressed. Moreover, in May 1965, the DPRK entered into a new military agreement with the Soviet Union that promised to bring a fresh flow of military hardware into North Korea.[13] Meanwhile, the PRC's guarded response to the U.S. military escalation in Vietnam did little to enhance Peking's sagging influence in Pyongyang.

THE SINO-KOREAN RIFT

Peking's reaction to Pyongyang's sudden turnabout was decidedly negative. In August 1965, in observance of the twentieth anniversary of the liberation of Korea, the Soviet Union elected to send a delegation led by Aleksandr N. Shelepin, a top policymaker, member of the Presidium and Secretariat, and Deputy Chairman of the Council of Ministers, while Peking chose to send a delegation led by Wu Hsin-yu, a Deputy Secretary General of the National People's Congress Standing Committee who was not even listed as a member of the CCP Central Committee at that time.

The period was marked by the heavy play given by the North Korean theoretical organs to chuche and the independent role played by the people of the DPRK in developing themselves. Pro forma references to the signal contributions made to the DPRK by Moscow and Peking that were usually observed on such occasions in the past, suddenly became a thing of the past. The major theme voiced by the Pyongyang media was that all successes and victories achieved, especially in the revolution, cannot be thought of apart from the course taken under the guidelines of chuche.

In August 1966, there was a further escalation in Sino-Korean differences. It occurred when the Peking media accused Pyongyang of being duped into collaboration with the "modern revisionists." The communique released at the end of the Eleventh Plenary Session of the Eighth Central Committee of the CCP contained the statement that:

> The Plenary Session maintains that to oppose imperialism, it is imperative to oppose modern revisionism. There is no middle road whatsoever in the struggle between Marxism-Leninism and modern revisionism. A clear line of demarcation must be drawn in dealing with modern revisionist groups with the leadership of the C.P.S.U. at the center and it is imperative to resolutely expose their true features as scabs. It is impossible to have "united action" with them.[14]

On the very day of the release of the Chinese communique, the Nodong Sinmun published a lengthy defense of the North Korean stand entitled "Let Us Defend Independence." The article emphasized that, "It is impermissible for a fraternal party to interfere in the policy of another party or bring pressure to bear on them." It added that:

> There can be no privileged party among the Communist and Workers' Parties. There are big parties and small ones, but there can be no superior party nor an inferior one, nor a party that gives guidance. There should be no such relations in

> which some issue orders and exercise control from a central post, while others obey and worship them from below. All are equally members of the international communist movement.[15]

As the Vietnam War was escalated and as the Great Proletarian Cultural Revolution was intensified by Red Guard activities, relations worsened between Pyongyang and Peking. Pyongyang's rejoinder to Peking's call for all parties to "draw a clear line of demarcation" between themselves and "modern revisionism" was to remind other parties, including the Chinese, that the issue of "whether to fight against U.S. imperialism or not" would be more appropriate for all parties to consider. As far as Pyongyang was concerned, the main issue was the united front in Vietnam.

> A large obstacle lies today in the way of realizing the anti-imperialist joint action and united front. There are serious differences and a lack of unity in the international communist movement which plays the vanguard role in the anti-imperialist struggle. The existing difficulties will not be settled of their own accord. The differences are serious, but we should sincerely explore ways and means of surmounting them. The situation urgently demands that we realize the anti-imperialist joint action. The materialization of the anti-imperialist joint action is the foremost and pressing revolutionary task confronting the socialist camp and the international communist movement. Whether to fight against U.S. imperialism or not, whether to support the revolutionary struggle of the world's people or not—these are the main points of the differences. The approach to these questions represents the touchstone for the appraisal of the Marxist-Leninist position of each party.[16]

Kim probably sympathized with Mao's domestic struggle to put down detractors favoring Soviet-assisted development for China over self-reliance. However, when the Vietnam controversy exacerbated the domestic conflict over the issue, it forced Mao to move up his timetable for purges envisaged originally under the Socialist education campaigns of the early 1960s. Mao's acceptance of Kim's united-front proposal of cooperating with the USSR in Vietnam would only have strengthened the hand of those in the Chinese power structure advocating Chinese development premised on cooperation with the USSR. In Pyongyang, where the domestic struggle was being waged over a guns-or-butter issue, the political threat to the strongly entrenched Kim was minimal compared to Mao. Therefore, once the Vietnam conflict threatened Korean interests, Kim's independence was ready to be expressed in the national interest and not necessarily in the interests of Mao's political survival. Thus, although Kim's ideological orientation was still much closer to Mao than to the Soviet leadership, the effect of Peking's excessive domestic preoccupation on the united front continued to trouble Kim. Concurrently, out of deference to Peking's right to its own domestic affairs, the Pyongyang media refrained from commenting on the Cultural Revolution except in highly oblique terms. Typically, for example, the North Koreans drew on a quote from Lenin to criticize the Chinese campaign.

> Proletarian culture is not something that has sprung from nobody knows whence; it is not an inventory of people who call themselves experts in proletarian culture. That is nonsense. Proletarian culture must be the result of a national development of the stores of knowledge which mankind has accumulated under the yoke of capitalist society, landlord society, bureaucratic society.[17]

In a separate commentary, without referring specifically to the Chinese, the North Korean media referred to the cultural revolution as an "extremely arduous and complex activity" requiring an enormous amount of effort over "a long period of time" by the working class that has seized the reins of power. It also added that, "This activity cannot be carried out with violence and however trying the task may be, it can only be brought about through patient education and indoctrination."[18]

North Korea's displeasure over the Chinese Cultural Revolution was also revealed in a commentary on "Trotskyism." The commentary was critical of "Trotskyites that set up an adventurist line in opposition to Marxist-Leninist principles" and their abuse of the "enterprise of youths to realize their counterrevolutionary purposes." It added that:

> Such Trotskyite activities separated the party from the masses, it deprived the party of a legal stage for the struggle and it ruined the revolutionary struggle. The Trotskyites' extreme

> subjectivity and "left" adventurism in strategy
> and tactics was present in the problem of the
> united front and of the unity in the activities of
> the working class and in the struggle for the liberation of the colonies which were allied with
> the proletarian revolution.[19]

While the North Koreans were disposed to regard "modern revisionism" as a continuing menace to the international communist movement they were more alarmed at "left opportunism," which prevented "a concentrated attack on the main enemy." As far as Kim Il-song was concerned, although the problems emanating from the Kremlin were disturbing, they at least held out the possibility of being resolved over the long run with changing world circumstances. As far as China's problems were concerned, however, there were immediate implications for the struggle in Vietnam, and ultimately for other Asian countries like Korea. Realizing Pyongyang's apprehensions and realizing the futility of trying to win the Koreans over immediately to their ideological fold, Moscow moved to undermine Chinese influence by preying on North Korea's anxieties. Through ringing declarations and military shipments to shore up the "defensive capabilities" of North Vietnam and North Korea, Moscow moved quickly to take advantage of the image of paralysis that had emerged out of China's preoccupation with its Cultural Revolution. The depth of Pyongyang's dilemma became evident as Sino-Korean differences spilled over into military matters. Ironically, Pyongyang found itself tracked on the military line of the deposed Peng Teh-huai, whose advocacy of military modernization backed by a flowing pipeline of Soviet arms and equipment was put down with the ascendancy of the Lin Piao line, predicated on Maoist guerrilla warfare principles and self-reliance.[20]

Meanwhile, Pyongyang continued to display its independence by balancing its criticism of China with criticism of Moscow. Pyongyang decried the ideological tendencies of "opportunists" to revise the contents "which constitute the core of Marxism-Leninism" to "suit the capitalists" and inflict "harmful distortions on the revolution." Both right-wing and left-wing opportunists were at fault according to North Korea.

> Special characteristics of right wing opportunism
> include the inability to stand firm on the class
> viewpoint, to surrender and compromise with
> imperialism and to negatively confront the reactionary struggle. Today, right wing opportunism is emerging as modern revisionism.

> The essential feature of left wing opportunism resembles that of right wing opportunism. The difference is that the left wing opportunists are ruining the revolution by veiling their own opportunistic actions with their own disturbing "revolutionary" language and by rashly turning out the masses for the revolution without even concrete reckoning.[21]

Kim Il-song's attempts to counsel bloc unity while preaching national independence proved to be both illusory and inconsistent. Either way there was no respite from the acrimonious crossfire that awaited Pyongyang every time it found itself forced between Moscow and Peking. Whereas the Chinese were quick to support North Korean independence whenever Pyongyang was threatened by Soviet domination, they were just as quick to condemn Pyongyang for being unduly independent of Chinese influence. The futility of seeking solace in principle was just as evident in Pyongyang's relations with Moscow as it was with Peking. The Pyongyang media's complaint was that, "One should not say that the policy of another party is all wrong or libel it at will because it does not conform to one's own policy."[22]

For ten years, the magnitude of Pyongyang's preoccupation with Moscow and Peking was reflected in its total lack of new relationships in the diplomatic area. In its first tentative steps to step out anew into the diplomatic world, the DPRK established relations with Cuba and Mali in 1960. In 1963, Yemen and the United Arab Republic (UAR) were added to the diplomatic list, and in 1964 the circle of relations was expanded to include Indonesia, Mauritania, Cambodia, Congo Brazzaville, and Ghana. In 1965, Tanzania was added.[23]

While North Korea's first entry into the diplomatic world was aided by the Soviet Union in 1948, in 1960 North Korean diplomany was aided by Peking. Within less than a year of Chou En-lai's much heralded trip through North Africa and sub-Saharan Africa in late 1963 and early 1964, Ch'oe Yong-kon, President of the DPRK Supreme People's Assembly followed a similar diplomatic route that took him to the UAR, Algeria, Mali, Guinea, and Ghana.[24] With Indonesia's Sukarno, Chou En-lai's main purpose was to arouse support for a second Afro-Asian Conference to counter the conferences of non-aligned nations from which China was being excluded.[25] However, the fall of the Ben Bella government, which prevented the Afro-Asian Conference from being held in Algeria; the abortive PKI coup in Indonesia; the military coups in Dahomey and Central Africa, which led to a severance of diplomatic relations with Peking by both countries and decisions by Burundi and Ghana to break relations with Peking, alerted the North Koreans to the immediate futility of following in

Peking's diplomatic tracks in the Third World. From Pyongyang's vantage point there was only one way to go--the independent way.

THE KOREAN WORKERS' PARTY CONFERENCE OF 1966

The despair in the DPRK over the state of bloc relations was evident at a rather unusual Party Conference convened in Pyongyang on October 5, 1966.[26] It was evident from Kim Il-song's opening statement to the Party Conference that the problems of the bloc were directly affecting Pyongyang.

> Comrades,
> The Korean revolution is a link in the whole chain of the world revolution and the revolutionary struggle of the Korean people is closely linked up with the struggle of the people of the whole world for peace and democracy, for national independence, and socialism.[27]

Within the year, Pyongyang had witnessed an aggravation rather than an improvement in the Sino-Soviet dispute, they had seen a "fraternal" Indonesian Communist Party as well as a friendly President Sukarno deposed by the Indonesian military, they had looked on with helplessness as a landmark ROK-Japan Treaty was being concluded, they had sensed increased threats to their own security with the escalation of the Vietnam War, and they had detected signs of a softening Soviet attitude toward Japan which, in the eyes of the North Koreans, again raised the specter of Japanese militarism.

In addition, it had become evident that the guns-and-butter policy adopted in Pyongyang had made severe inroads on the country's economic development, prompting a three-year extension of the DPRK Seven-Year Plan, which had been scheduled for completion in 1967. One of the underlying reasons for Pyongyang's impressive economic performances following the Korean War was that the DPRK had been relatively free of heavy military outlays. Once the policy of economic development in parallel with military upbuilding was adopted, the economic picture changed completely. Besides, Kim admitted in his report at the Conference that unity had not been achieved between the Communist and Workers' Parties and that the state of affairs had affected "revolution and construction" in North Korea.[28]

The North Korean media coverage of the Party Conference was sketchy as usual but the fact that a Party Conference was called instead of a Party Congress enabled Pyongyang to exclude all foreign observers, indicating that sensitive issues were raised. A significant indication was provided at the Fourteenth Plenary Session of the Fourth Party Central Committee, which was held immediately after the Party Conference to legitimize a new leadership alignment.[29]

The cult of Kim Il-song emerged with the support of the new political alignment of Party loyalists. It had become obvious to Kim that Marxism-Leninism was less successful in providing ready solutions to differences among fraternal countries than the rationale for the more gainful task of haranguing "imperialism." Kim believed, therefore, that Marxist-Leninist solutions to Korean problems could only be achieved through positive leadership, which he stood ready to exercise. Like some of the other militant leaders of the smaller countries, Kim came to look upon the Soviet policy apparatus as having grown into conventionality in its relations with the West, and had become increasingly nonmilitant, conservative, and bureaucratic at a time when the Chinese policy apparatus was mired in its own Red Guard-inspired upheavals.

It was a self-assured Kim Il-song, confident of his political omnipotence at home and reassured of his "greatness" even on the international front by a willing and well-schooled mass media, who took it upon himself to speak out for the increasingly dispossessed "small" countries of the bloc. Few leaders had a better tooled political apparatus or a better indoctrinated mass base to draw on. The new line that emerged was a self-reliant Korean way attuned to the realities of polycentrism within the bloc and based on the belief that loyalty to higher ideals could only be defined and achieved in terms of loyalty to Kim Il-song. In other words, loyalty to the Party or the state must first be channeled through Kim Il-song. According to the Party media, "The most fundamental characteristic of a Communist revolutionary is loyalty to the leader," and "the task of turning the revolutionary ideology of Comrade Kim Il-song" into a "resolute faith that is part of our flesh and bones is our foremost revolutionary responsibility."[30]

Following the Party Conference, efforts were stepped up to provide Kim Il-song with instant recognition as "one of the outstanding leaders of the international Communist movement" and to put forth his views on revolution as models for revolution in the small countries of the bloc and the countries of the Third World.

The Party Conference marked North Korea's move back to the middle as a nonaligned country. The policy of nonalignment was not fully in keeping with the desires of Moscow but it represented a vast improvement over the state of relations that had prevailed during the Khrushchev era. Perhaps the most symbolic act in the easing of relations was in the Soviet-Korean trade agreement concluded on June 20, 1966, which placed trade relations between the two countries back on a long-term basis.[31] Among other things, it gained the DPRK Soviet assistance in the construction of a thermal power plant and an oil refinery, and aid to enlarge the capacity of a major steel complex. The trade agreement, plus a separate military agreement, came in the aftermath of Soviet economic reprisals for North Korea's espousal of the Chinese line during the height of the Sino-Soviet dispute.

Meanwhile, the shift away from the Chinese line drew the displeasure of Peking even though the shift was prompted by North Korea's national interest. The threat to its national security felt in Pyongyang was quite real and while the guerrilla tactics employed by Kim in the fabled "anti-Japanese struggle" and by Mao in China were integral to such "national liberation struggles," it was obvious to Pyongyang that such tactics would be of little avail in the rugged and barren terrain in Korea where pitched battles and massive frontal assaults from fixed positions had been the rule rather than the exception in the Korean War. Thus, given the option, Kim Il-song had no qualms about accepting Soviet concepts and firepower as alternatives to a complete reliance on Maoist concepts for defensive warfare.

As Kim Il-song's personality cult blossomed in Pyongyang and as the frustrations of bloc disunity began to weigh increasingly on the North Korean leadership, radical political alternatives became increasingly attractive to the restive DPRK regime. As the North Korean propaganda apparatus began to tout Kim Il-song as the first great leader to bring the United States to its knees in a war, the growing myth of invincibility began to accelerate the trend toward recklessness. Kim was ready to emerge as an international political activist in his own right but the risks deemed appropriate by Kim were soon to dismay even the hardliners in Moscow and Peking.

THE RADICAL TURN AND THE UNIFICATION ISSUE

According to Kim Il-song, the unification of Korea "brooks no delay." Yet, unification is the one major goal that has eluded him. He failed to achieve it through the Korean War. By his own account, North Korea missed an opportunity to exploit the instability in the South when the Syngman Rhee government was being brought down in Seoul. When the Pak Chong-hui government gook over in the South, the odds for a Northern takeover of the South declined drastically. The brutal episode of the Korean War, which left a lingering aversion to Communist aggression in the South and a shared appreciation of the return to normalcy with positive signs of economic betterment, helped President Pak Chong-hui to bring stability to the South just as conditions in the North were beginning to take a downward turn.

Beginning in 1964, South Korea's Gross National Product began to grow at a rapid 12 percent rate annually, and equally impressive gains were registered in foreign trade and industrial production.[32] In South Korea, the direct involvement of 50,000 troops in combat in South Vietnam plus the engagement of thousands of civilians in noncombat, support-type operations boosted its national pride and economic prosperity. The propaganda dividends for the South were a comforting self-image and a source of international prestige at the expense of the North. The DPRK, meanwhile, remained tied to a policy pronouncement that expressed a willingness to furnish combat troops to the Vietnamese National Liberation Front and North Vietnam "if requested."[33]

As the ROK contribution to the war effort in Vietnam grew in significance, the North Koreans felt their own sense of global esteem diminishing. It also made unification on their terms even more remote. While Pyongyang had furnished material aid to the Vietcong and the North Vietnamese and while there were reports of North Korean pilots flying sorties in Vietnam, the North Korean regime clearly felt that it needed to do more to counter ROK gains on the international scene. With no hope for the development of a militant united front of Communist bloc forces in Vietnam and with ROK troops fitting increasingly well into the alignment of forces against the Vietcong, a dramatic turnabout was felt to be needed to assuage Pyongyang's wounded pride.

If there was a time when Kim Il-song could count on support for military action within the Political Committee, it was in 1966. The leadership realignment that occurred following the Party Conference placed men of strong military backgrounds and biases into the key party slots.*

The radical turn in North Korean policy came with two almost simultaneous incidents. On January 21, 1968, 34 members of an elite North Korean guerrilla unit attempted to assassinate President Pak Chong-hui at the official Blue House residence in Seoul.[34] The North Korean team of assassins was stopped just 500 meters short of the presidential compound. During the uproar that followed, naval units of the North Korean People's Army then pulled off another surprise attack by seizing the USS Pueblo off the coast of Wonsan.

The North Korean newspapers began by giving far more prominent front-page coverage to the attempted assassination of President Pak than to the seizure of the Pueblo. The newspapers had apparently

---

*A key shift was the replacement of Yi Hyo-sun, a ranking Party member, by General Ho Pong-hak as the head of the Liaison Bureau, which was charged with operations against the South.

hoped to portray the incident as an attempted assassination by revolutionary groups within South Korea. When that failed, media coverage switched immediately to the Pueblo incident.

The world response to the event varied. The ROK military was ready to retaliate immediately but was restrained by the United States. In Moscow, the response was guarded. The incident was reported a day later but only as a Korean Central News Agency (KCNA) report. The East European countries similarly reacted with caution. Peking maintained silence on the incident until January 25. However, unlike the Kremlin, Peking elected to release a statement of support for the seizure. The formal government statement was released on January 28, 1968.

The most enthusiastic support for Kim Il-song's action came from the North Vietnamese and the Cubans. The North Vietnamese rejoiced over the diversion and the U.S. humiliation, and saw the act as a contribution to the Vietnamese war effort.

It is unlikely that the Soviets instigated the seizure of the Pueblo. In fact, Moscow suffered virtually the same fate some months later when 52 Soviet crewmen and two fishing trawlers were seized by a Ghanaian Navy corvette for "violating Ghanaian territorial waters."[35]

On the other hand, in view of their strained relations, it is also unlikely that Peking encouraged the seizure of the Pueblo. Actually, Pyongyang's perception of Peking's attitude toward Kim Il-song worsened with the appearance of defamatory Red Guard publications. According to one:

> Kim Il-song is an out-and-out counter-revolutionary revisionist as well as a millionaire, an aristocrat, and a leading member of the bourgeoisie. His main residence in Pyongyang is a beautiful, capitalistic-type mansion surrounded on all sides by sentry posts. He also owns six country estates paid for by the people whom he exploits and on which he employs the services of large numbers of security personnel.[36]

The other possibility of a bloc-wide effort to undermine the United States in Asia was also unlikely in view of the fragmented state of bloc affairs at that time. In short, the responsibility for the seizure pointed to the North Korean leadership. The heady atmosphere that prevailed in Pyongyang in the aftermath of the two incidents and the ascendancy of the militant viewpoint in the policy councils of the DPRK was particularly evident at the twentieth anniversary celebrations marking the founding of the Korean People's Army on February 8, 1968, just two weeks after the seizure of the Pueblo.[37]

Following Kim Il-song's call at the Party Conference to "step up the revolutionary struggle" in the South, a new pattern of infiltration began against the South. Northern infiltration teams bent on establishing revolutionary bases in remote areas began to replace single operatives targeted against the urban areas.[38] The pattern of infiltrations also began to resemble the tactics employed by North Vietnamese against Saigon, with Pyongyang serving as the "base of revolution" for the revolution in the South.

A consideration in Kim Il-song's decision to resort to subversion, terrorism, and piracy was to relieve North Vietnam by diverting some of the pressure away from it. But in doing so and in insisting that all countries of the bloc join in defeating the United States in Vietnam they only succeeded in further alienating the Chinese, who were opposed to any form of cooperation with the Soviet Union. Nor was Mao under any compulsion to follow the dictates of the upstart Korean ruler. At the same time, the Soviet Union was reluctant to go beyond furnishing material aid and support to Hanoi. It must have become evident to Kim that united action in Vietnam was not forthcoming within the Socialist camp. It was under those circumstances that the Pueblo was seized in January 1968.

Kim was quick to prey on the American predicament. By holding the U.S. crewmen hostage, he was able to rely on U.S. restrictions against ROK military retaliation to insure his immediate security. As Pyongyang moved to reap propaganda benefits from the incident, the United States moved to beef-up the ROK military establishment with up-to-date hardware that included F-4 Phantom jets, heavy tanks, and naval warcraft. Moreover, instead of exacerbating the domestic problems that were beginning to trouble the Pak government in Seoul and spreading panic, the incidents had a catalytic effect in uniting the country even more firmly around Seoul. With the aid of Israeli counterinsurgency experts and U.S. assistance, an extensive local militia network was established to counter further threats from the North. Moreover, the incidents provided Seoul with better levers to pry further military assistance from the United States.

The first break in the disposition of the captured American crewmen thus came from Pyongyang. In welcoming a Rumanian Party delegation to Pyongyang, Kim Kwang-hyop, a ranking Party member, pointed out that "there is precedent for the treatment of similar cases at the Korean Armistice Commission," on January 31, 1968.[39] The statement indicated that Pyongyang was willing to negotiate at Panmunjom.

As the talks dragged on at Panmunjom, problems began to loom for Pyongyang. By announcing on March 31, 1968, that he would not seek reelection in the upcoming U.S. presidential elections, President

PERILS OF INDEPENDENCE

Lyndon Johnson left Pyongyang with the option of accepting his offer or the offer of an unpredictable U.S. administration at some future point in time. It was under those circumstances that an agreement was reached for the release of the Pueblo crewmen.

Kim Il-song's perception of the U.S. strategy was that it was intent on destroying "the small countries one by one, while refraining from worsening its relations with the big powers."[40] Kim therefore emerged from the Pueblo incident confident that:

> If more countries, even if small, pool their strength and fight resolutely against imperialism, the people can knock down U.S. imperialism with decisively overwhelming power at each and every front. The peoples of all countries making revolution should tear the limbs off of the U.S. beast and behead it all over the world. The U.S. imperialists appear to be strong but when the peoples of many countries attack them from all sides and join in mutilating them in that way, they will soon become impotent and bite the dust in the end.[41]

During his own era of militancy, Kim was obviously attracted to the Cuban revolutionary line, which he referred to as a "lighthouse of hope" for Latin America, and also to the Vietcong struggle, which sought to preface the final political showdown with military assaults. Kim applied the same Vietcong tactics to the militant portion of his unification line. The pro-Cuban and the pro-Vietcong biases may have been reinforced by the Pueblo incident, which again demonstrated to Kim that the Russians and the Chinese were far more concerned about their own national interests than the interests of the small countries.

The culmination of Pyongyang's radical line came with the shooting down of an American EC-121 reconnaissance aircraft by fighter planes of the Korean People's Army (KPA) 896th Unit on April 15, 1969, which also happened to be Kim Il-song's fifty-seventh birthday. This time, the United States was in a position to devastate Pyongyang with air and naval strikes. U.S. restraint may have been aided considerably by obvious signs of displeasure over North Korean actions in both Moscow and Peking.

The immediate Soviet reaction to the incident was to send its own naval units to aid the American naval search for survivors. The Chinese, who were by then involved in their own tense border confrontation with the Russians, were similarly perturbed by the incident and the limits to which the cult of Kim Il-song had been carried.

In apparent reference to the rising cult of Kim Il-song one source reported that:

> The Chinese protested privately the last time the Kim cult over-stepped the bounds. Advertisements appeared a few years ago in Western newspapers billing the Beloved Leader as "the greatest thinker-theoretician Asia has ever produced." A sharp word from Peking produced swift modifications. Kim Il-song was merely proclaimed "One of the greatest. . . ."[42]

With millions of Soviet troops poised along its own borders, Peking could hardly allow the disturbances along its eastern flank to go untended. The first step in curbing Pyongyang's excesses was to improve state relations between the PRC and the DPRK. The first sign of a thaw came when the DPRK dispatched a high-ranking delegation led by Supreme People's Assembly (SPA) President Ch'oe Yong-kon to the celebrations commemorating the twentieth anniversary of the founding of the PRC. It was the first faint sign of Pyongyang's return to moderation in its foreign relations.

NOTES

1. Chester L. Cooper, The Lost Crusade: America in Vietnam (New York: Dodd, Mead, 1970), pp. 487-88.
2. Nodong Sinmun, February 12, 1965.
3. Quoted in "North Korea's Neutral Course," a paper prepared by the Research Department of Radio Free Europe, August 25, 1965.
4. The U.S. bombing of North Vietnam was launched after the attack on Pleiku. President Johnson indicated that further developments would depend on the Communist response, indicating that Kosygin, who also announced Soviet willingness to aid Hanoi if invaded, was probably aware of possible North Vietnamese plans to step up the dispatch of regular units to the South. U.S., Congress, Senate, Committee on Foreign Relations, Background Information Relating to Southeast Asia and Vietnam (Washington, D.C.: U.S. Government Printing Office, 1970), p. 19.
5. Kim Il-song, Selected Works, vol. 2 (Pyongyang: Foreign Languages Publishing House, 1965), pp. 515-16.
6. Ibid., p. 525.
7. Ibid., p. 527.
8. Ibid., p. 537.

9. Kim stated that, ". . . Because of the fact that we had to direct great efforts to the further strengthening of our defense capacities to cope with the situation obtaining in the last two or three years, the economic development of our country was subsequently retarded to some extent when compared with the plan." Ibid., p. 519.

10. <u>Minju Choson</u>, November 24, 1965.

11. <u>Tass</u>, February 8, 1965.

12. The North Koreans accused the United States of using the treaty as a first step toward the creation of a "Northeast Asian Treaty Organization." <u>Nodong Sinmun</u>, October 2, 1965.

13. Henry S. Chang, "Plans and Starts," <u>Far Eastern Economic Review</u> 55, no. 3 (January 19, 1967): 94.

14. <u>Peking Review</u>, no. 34, August 19, 1966, p. 7.

15. <u>Nodong Sinmun</u>, August 12, 1966.

16. Ibid.

17. Ibid.

18. <u>Nodongja Sinmun</u>, December 15, 1966.

19. <u>Nodong Sinmun</u>, September 15, 1966.

20. Lin Piao, "Long Live the Victory of the People's War," <u>Peking Review</u>, no. 36, September 3, 1965, pp. 9-30.

21. <u>Nodongja Sinmun</u>, January 28, 1967.

22. <u>Nodong Sinmun</u>, August 12, 1966.

23. Korean Central News Agency, <u>Korean Central Yearbook</u>, 1965, pp. 123-25.

24. Ibid., pp. 530-31.

25. Harold C. Hinton, <u>China's Turbulent Quest: An Analysis of China's Foreign Relations Since 1945</u> (New York: Macmillan Co., 1970), pp. 146-47.

26. According to Party rules, the Central Committee of the Party has the right to convene, when necessary, the Party Conference in the intervals between Party Congresses. The Party Conference discusses urgent problems relating to the policy and tactics of the Party, and has the right to recall members of the Central Committee who failed to fulfill their duties and replace or elect them anew. <u>Third Congress of the Workers' Party of Korea: Documents and Materials</u> (Pyongyang, 1956), p. 398.

27. Pyongyang <u>Times</u> (Supplement), October 13, 1966.

28. Ibid.

29. Members of the Political Committee: Kim Il-song, Ch'oe Yong-kon, Kim Il, Pak Kum-ch'ol, Yi Hyo-sun, Kim Kwang-hyop, Kim Ik-son, Kim Ch'ang-poing, Pak Song-ch'ol, Ch'oe Hyon, Yi Yong-ho. Candidate Members: Sok San, Ho Pong-hak, Ch'oe Kwang, O Chin-u, Yim Ch'un-ch'u, Kim Tong-kyu, Kim Yong-chu, Pak Yong-kuk, Chong Kyong-pok. <u>Nodong Sinmun</u>, October 13, 1966. The

strength of personal, group, and regional ties, evident in the new line-up, cannot be overestimated in Korean politics. At least 11 and probably more of the permanent and candidate members belonged to Kim's old Kapsan faction, made up of men who fought together in Manchuria and then escaped to the Soviet Union. At least 8 of the top 11 members were from North Hamgyong Province and most were either educated in Russia or formerly involved in Soviet affairs. Also, most were men with military backgrounds.

30. Nodong Sinmun, August 2, 1974.

31. Korean Central News Agency, Korean Central Yearbook, 1966-67, p. 507.

32. Morton Abramowitz, "Moving the Glacier: The Two Koreas and the Powers," Adelphi Papers, no. 80 (London: International Institute for Strategic Studies, September 1971), p. 2.

33. In a speech delivered at the Party Conference on October 5, 1966, Kim Il-song stated that, "We are preparing to send our volunteers to join the Vietnamese brothers and sisters in their battles whenever requested by the Government of the Democratic Republic of Vietnam . . . ." Pyongyang Times (Supplement), October 13, 1966.

34. In mid-1972, Kim Il-song was reported to have apologized to ROK representatives for the attempted assassination of Pak, blaming "extreme leftists" for it. Choson Ilbo, February 28, 1974.

35. Korea Times, February 19, 1969.

36. Parade, Supplement to the Washington Post, July 14, 1968. A more detailed account is contained in Wen-ko T'ung-hsun (Cultural Revolution Bulletin), no. 11 (February 15, 1968).

37. On Army Day, the DPRK's highest military awards were conferred on six of North Korea's top military officers--five of whom were candidate members of the Political Committee. They were Kim Chang-pong, Vice Premier of the Cabinet and Minister of National Defense; Sok San, Minister of Public Security; Ho Pong-hak, Secretary of the Central Committee of the KWP; Ch'oe Kwang, Chief of the General Staff of the KPS; O Chin-u, Director of the General Political Bureau of the KPA; and O Paek-ryong, Vice Minister of National Defense. Pyongyang Times, February 15, 1968.

38. Prisoner interrogations revealed that at least 8,000 personnel were being trained for guerrilla operations against the South. Sources also revealed the presence of guerrilla training centers for foreign nationals under the Ministry of National Defense. David Rees, "North Korea's Growth as a Subversive Center," Conflict Studies, no. 28 (November 1972): 8.

39. Korean Central News Agency broadcast, January 31, 1968.

40. Nodong Sinmun, November 21, 1968.

41. Ibid.

42. Far Eastern Economic Review, August 16, 1974, p. 5.

CHAPTER 6

CONTROLLED MODERATION AND DETENTE: 1970-75

The cult of Kim Il-song, which was synonymous with the radicalization of the late 1960s, fed on success but often success fed on opportunism simply because service to Kim was confused with service to the state. In 1968, the rewriting of history was carried further to credit Kim's mother and father as true progenitors of Korea's revolutionary tradition. Simultaneously, the North Korean press also highlighted the revolutionary role of Kim Chong-suk, deceased first wife of Kim Il-song, who bore him the son who is now the subject of speculation as Kim's eventual successor. It may very well be that the historical legitimization of Kim Chong-suk conferred the political legitimacy that her son, Kim Chong-il needed to cut his political teeth in the era of radicalism when others were purged for their errors. In essence, however, the cult was pushed to its most frenzied height because the hawks that dominated the doves within the Political Committee found it to their advantage to support the cult and work through it rather than around it.

In the heady era of "independence," to believe in chuche was to believe in Kim's way, and the radicalism that supported Kim on that path thrived on resentment. At home, it fed on resurrected class resentments; abroad, on the bitterness of "small-country" resentment. In a country with a poverty of classical intellectual enterprise and hordes of new Socialist-bred "intellectuals" trained and indoctrinated for technocracy and unremitting loyalty to the state, Kim emerged as a willing national symbol of guidance for the aggrieved. His demagoguery reflected his egalitarianism: to uplift the masses at home and to manipulate great power disagreements at a more manageable level abroad. To Kim, such acts as piracy on the high seas and in the air over Korea seemed justifiable to dramatize the depths of Pyongyang's resentments to a world that seemed oblivious

to his beliefs. Kim soon learned, however, that Moscow's annoyance
over his obstruction of U.S.-USSR detente was increasingly being
shared by Peking. Peking's concern was particularly heightened by
the Soviet invasion of Czechoslovakia in August 1968, which increased
the possibility of a Soviet invasion of China. In Peking, the lessons
of the Brezhnev Doctrine added to its concern over the diminishing
U.S. presence in Asia. The Nixon Doctrine was seen as an opening
wedge for Soviet hegemony in Asia. It was not difficult for Peking
to believe that the Kremlin would be inclined to treat the sovereignty
of the Asian countries with the same contempt that it showed for the
East European countries. It was under those circumstances that
Chinese Premier Chou-En-lai flew to Pyongyang on April 5, 1970,
in an attempt to restore Sino-Korean relations and to enjoin Pyongyang to take a more moderate course.[1]

THE CHOU EN-LAI VISIT TO PYONGYANG

As the DPRK prepared to receive its first high ranking PRC
visitor to Pyongyang since 1963, an evaluation of North Korea's own
stand was in order. Pyongyang's main concern was the Sino-Soviet
dispute and it was time to look again at the balance sheet.

On the Soviet side of the ledger, Pyongyang regarded the
Brezhnev regime a definite improvement over the Khrushchev regime. There were still issues separating Moscow and Pyongyang but
there were less intrusions and the Koreans, unlike the Chinese, were
willing to wait and see prior to making judgments about the Kremlin.
Pyongyang still opposed the line of peaceful coexistence but much of
the harshness formerly evident in their criticism was toned down in
light of Moscow's renewed support of national liberation movements,
which had previously languished under Khrushchev. Other issues included Pyongyang's fear of the implications of Soviet labor liberalization practices for its own militant program of Socialist construction;
it resented Moscow's conventional UN role, which provided implicit
support for the UN Command in Korea; it resented the Soviet reluctance to openly criticize the Sato government and Soviet efforts to engage the Japanese in industrial joint ventures in Siberia. Moscow's
increasingly circumspect attitude toward France and West Germany
and the respectful treatment accorded deGaulle during the French
leader's visit to Moscow disturbed the Koreans, who felt that the
USSR and the Warsaw Pact nations should be doing more to step up
pressures in Europe to lessen U.S. pressures against the Asian
countries.

On the Chinese side of the ledger, Pyongyang objected to Peking's attempt to justify its left adventurist excesses solely on grounds

of opposition to Soviet revisionism. The North Koreans were even more incensed at Chinese attempts to force their views on the Koreans. Peking's impatience with Pyongyang's inclination to view Khrushchev's downfall and Brezhnev's ascendancy as a possible portent of improving bloc relations rather than as a continuation of the revisionist line was tried even further by Pyongyang's efforts to improve its relations with Moscow. To the worried Koreans, the virulence of the Chinese anti-Soviet attitude was no different than the anti-Soviet attitude of the imperialists, with the result that it had become increasingly difficult to separate the issue of confronting imperialism from the issues governing bloc relations. The heightened tensions within the bloc had, in fact, raised the distinct possibility of a Sino-Soviet war. Peking's intransigence on the united-front issue in Vietnam was particularly disturbing to Pyongyang since it felt that continued Soviet aid to Vietnam at least provided better prospects for the eventual eradication of revisionism than any amount of Chinese haranguing. Nor was Pyongyang well disposed toward the Chinese argument that the bloc was going through an inevitable phase of divisiveness. Finally, the setbacks suffered by the North Koreans themselves in emulating such grand socialist experiments as the Great Leap Forward convinced Pyongyang of the merits of sober and planned development.[2]

Chou En-lai's visit to Pyongyang was preceded by a return to normalized diplomatic relations between Peking and Pyongyang. In February 1970, Hyon Chun-kuk returned to the post that he had vacated as DPRK Ambassador to the PRC in September 1967.[3] Then on March 23, 1970, Li Yun-chuan was assigned as the first PRC Ambassador to the DPRK since mid-1967.

An innate cautiousness was evident on both sides as Chou En-lai arrived in Pyongyang to begin his visit. In speeches delivered at the airport, both Kim Il-song and Chou En-lai chose to emphasize the only issue upon which there was a unanimity of interest, and that was their shared antipathy for Japan and the United States. Kim referred to the people of both countries as "close comrade-in-arms and brothers who have fought shoulder to shoulder" against "Japanese militarism and U.S. imperialism, the common enemies."[4] Chou likewise referred to the two countries as having relations of "lips to teeth" and accused the United States and Japan of colluding in directing "the spearhead of aggression" against countries like China and Korea.[5] The same theme was emphasized throughout Chou's stay in North Korea as both sides publicly shunned the ideological issues and refrained from criticizing Moscow. The pointed attack on the Sato government may have been in response to the Sato-Nixon talks of November 1969, which provided for the reversion of Okinawa to Japan and a reaffirmation of support for the U.S.-Japan Security Treaty.

At the same time, the anti-Japanese attitude may have been a reminder to the Soviets of the perils of dealing with the Japanese.

Otherwise, the fact that a muted silence was maintained on the issues of the bloc indicated that there was little agreement between the two sides on the ideological issues of the Sino-Soviet dispute, which were undoubtedly discussed in private. However, the mere fact that Chou was able to bring about an improvement in relations was a positive step forward for Peking. It could at least count on North Korean neutrality in the event of a Soviet invasion and it at least increased Peking's leverage in pressuring Moscow for negotiations rather than open conflict.

By refusing to cave in to any major Chinese demands, Kim Il-song managed to preserve and to even increase his independence. The complete lack of criticism against "modern revisionism" kept his options with Moscow open and the fact that a hijacked Japan Airlines plane was promptly returned to Japan on April 5 indicates that Pyongyang was not eager to close its doors to Japan in spite of its hostility to the Sato government.[6] Moreover, Pyongyang could not have been unaware of the growing volume of trade between Peking and Tokyo and of the talks being conducted between the Americans and the Chinese in Warsaw. In other words, both sides were reluctant to cede options that would prevent them from dealing independently with the enemies that they had joined in condemning.

Pyongyang's adherence to its flexible diplomacy was demonstrated within weeks of Chou En-lai's departure from Pyongyang. On April 28, 1970, Kim Il-song received Marshal Zakharov, Chief of the General Staff of the Soviet Army and First Deputy Minister of Defense, who was on a visit to the DPRK at the invitation of the Korean People's Army.[7] The timing of Zakharov's visit was noteworthy since the last high-ranking Soviet military delegation to visit Pyongyang was in 1965, soon after the Kosygin visit and after which there was a significant upgrading of the North Korean military defense forces. This time, however, as indicated by the cordial but obviously "correct" relations that marked Soviet Politburo member and Deputy Premier Mazurov's visit to Pyongyang in August 1970, for the twenty-fifth anniversary observances of DPRK independence, there was no comparable military upgrading in the offing. The Soviet response was in keeping with their refusal to support Kim Il-song's seizure of the USS Pueblo and the shooting down of the EC-121. It was also probably an indication of Pyongyang's negative response to Soviet proposals for an Asian collective security system. However, the Soviet presence in Pyongyang was probably designed also to prevent a Soviet-perceived Chinese instigation of Korean adventurism and to see to it that the U.S. phaseout from Asia would not lead to any rash acts that would draw the USSR into any dangerous confrontation with the United States.

There were clear indications in the North Korean press that Sino-Korean relations had once again ascended over Soviet-Korean relations. Messages from the leadership in Peking that had been given second billing in the press until 1969 were suddenly given top billing in 1970. Moreover, the highly honorific terms used to address the Chinese leadership compared to the more conventional terms used to refer to the Soviet leadership, whose messages were relegated to second billing, indicated to the Party members and the North Korean masses that the Chinese were being favored by Kim Il-song. The Chou visit ended a period of ill-feeling punctuated by DPRK accusations of Chinese meddling in its domestic affairs, including the rumor floated by Peking of the purge of KWP Political Committee member and Vice-Premier Kim Kwang-hyop, Red Guard posters referring to Kim Il-song as a "fat revisionist," and reports of sporadic border clashes between Chinese and Korean troops along the Sino-Korean border.

THE FIFTH PARTY CONGRESS: PLANS FOR AN UNCERTAIN FUTURE

The Fifth Congress of the KWP opened on November 2, 1970, with the North Koreans still saddled with the problem of dealing with "fraternal" countries (the USSR and PRC) that persisted in being enemies. To avoid the touchy issue of representation, no foreign guests were invited to the opening session of the Congress. As Kim Il-song prepared to sum up the results of the Seven-Year Plan, which took nearly ten years to complete, it was obvious that Pyongyang needed assurances of a stability of relations in all quarters of the Socialist camp rather than in any one country to pursue its new six-year economic development plan. It was obvious to Pyongyang that its performance under the next economic development plan would depend greatly on the nature of its foreign relations.[8] Although by the late 1960s the DPRK had begun to expand its base of relationships with other countries, its record of past economic performances indicated that strong reliance would still have to be placed on Moscow and Peking as trading partners.[9]

By 1970, however, Sino-Soviet tensions had not abated and there was no sign of conciliation in either Moscow or Peking as each side sought to claim the mantle of leadership in the world revolution. Moreover, in Moscow, there was an obvious determination to thwart China's bid to obstruct Brezhnev's drive toward detente with nations such as the United States and Japan. In 1968, Brezhnev provided stark proof of his willingness to employ the naked power of the Soviet Army to crush any threatening signs of heresy within the bloc. Mao Tse-tung responded by condemning the Soviet invasion of

Czechoslovakia. The North Koreans, like the Cubans, whose relations with Moscow had also cooled because of Castro's independent support of Latin American revolutionary movements, were more guarded in their response. While Cuba was willing to concede that the invasion was politically necessary, though legally unnecessary, Pyongyang seemed content merely to cite the unfortunate consequences of revisionism in Czechoslovakia.

> The revisionist policy that has been pursued in Czechoslovakia finds concentric manifestation particularly in giving up the class struggle and denying the dictatorship of the proletariat. To deny the class struggle and the dictatorship of the proletariat is the anti-Marxist, counter-revolutionary essence of revisionism.[10]

There were two facets to the Korean response. The criticism of Czech revisionism was practically indistinguishable from North Korea's past criticism of Soviet revisionism. Pyongyang seemed willing to go so far as to criticize Czech revisionism as surrogate Soviet revisionism. But it was reluctant to openly criticize the Soviet invasion. This allowed the North Koreans to balance their criticism of revisionism with what the Kremlin could accept as tacit North Korean support for Brezhnev's actions in Prague. Furthermore, while Mao was compelled by the event to counsel the Chinese people to eschew any search for "hegemony," Kim's response to this day has been to back away from this issue.

In spite of the noticeable chill in Soviet-Korean relations, the DPRK was careful not to exceed the parameters of Soviet acceptability. Given that understanding, Moscow seemed willing to give Pyongyang a certain amount of leeway as long as a continuation of state relations provided mutual benefits and accessibility should a future accommodation of views materialize into closer relations. The persistence of the Sino-Soviet split into the 1970s assured Pyongyang of some hope of pursuing an independent course between the two contending enemies.

The first step in the new drive for total mobilization began with a restructuring of the Party leadership under Kim. The new Political Committee alignment assured Kim Il-song of a working consensus at the top of the Party apparatus.[11] Each member of the Political Committee was accountable in some manner to Kim Il-song and, with the possible exception of Kim Chung-nin, each had already proven his loyalty to Kim during the anti-Japanese struggle in Manchuria. The change in the Political Committee lineup reflected the change in priorities at the Fifth Party Congress. Members missing from the

MODERATION AND DETENTE

1966 Political Committee included those associated with the military adventurism, the anti-South strategy, and the economic failures of the late 1960s.*

Scalapino and Lee have noted that from the Fourth Party Congress in 1961 to the Fifth Party Congress in 1970, over two-thirds of the Party elite disappeared as a result of purges, deaths, and other causes. Moreover, the presence of long-standing associates of Kim Il-song and the presence of a liberal sprinkling of relatives both within the Central Committee and the government indicate that cronyism and nepotism contributed heavily to the membership selection.[12] Also, the continued presence of the military as a numerically dominant group within the Central Committee assured Kim that trusted members would continue to serve as conduits to a traditional source of power.

The nature of the Central Committee membership seemed to accord with some of the concerns expressed by Kim in his report to the Party delegates. He reaffirmed North Korea's determination to continue on an independent course with the support of a Party that had rid itself of foreign influences. Kim's reference to the heavy inroads made by defense spending on economic development, and the need to rely more realistically on the revolutionary views and tactics popularized during the anti-Japanese struggle indicated that there would be no overwhelming tilt toward a military posture geared to the sophisticated and expensive hardware of the rich nations. The emphasis would continue to be on arming "the entire nation" to create a vast militia system. His remarks also underscored the need for the people of South Korea to mount their own revolution, indicating that North Korea would not rely on the heavy infiltration tactics and terrorism used in the late 1960s.

Armed with renewed support within the Political Committee, Kim served notice on all potential dissidents that the polarization that led to the emergence of "extreme leftists" and economic "revisionists" within the Party between 1966 and 1968 would not be tolerated. It also seemed to indicate that foreign aggression as a focal point of overriding concern would be replaced by a concern for internal subversion by responsible officials enamored of foreign or capitalist-leaning views. Kim Il-song's deep concern over the problems of

---

*The "extreme leftists" responsible for the military adventurism probably included Kim Ch'ang-pong, Ho Pong-hak, and Ch'oe Kwang. Those connected with the anti-South strategy and internal security probably included Yi Hyo-sun, Pak Yong-kuk, Chong Kyong-pok, and Sok San. The proponents of "revisionist" economic views were probably Yi Hyo-sun and Pak Kum-ch'ol.

domestic mobilization welled to the surface within weeks of the close of the Fifth Party Congress when worker riots over rising food prices triggered events that led to the downfall of Gomulka in Poland in December 1970.

In a manner reminiscent of their handling of the Czech uprising in August 1968, the North Korean media never once mentioned Poland or the Soviet Union in their condemnation of the events that transpired in Poland. The article, which appeared under the title "Let Us Uphold the Dictatorship of the Proletariat and Proletarian Democracy" agonized over the harmful effect that revisionism had on "some countries" within the Communist bloc. In a pointed reminder to the "modern revisionists" the article emphasized that:

> If the class character of proletarian democracy is denied and everyone is given freedom to speak and act as he pleases under socialism, this would mean granting the counter-revolutionaries and the anti-socialist elements "freedom" to maneuver unhindered and bring bourgeois democracy into socialist society. The complicated situation caused in some socialist countries of late is a result of having thrown away the dictatorship of the proletariat and of having allowed bourgeois democracy in after loud cries for their so-called "pure democracy" and "complete liberty."[13]

The policy of deliberate obfuscation fit in with calculated efforts to suppress all news relating to such developments within the DPRK. Liberalization anywhere, and particularly at home, was anathema to the Kim regime. Kim's main concern, of course, was the corrosive effects of "democracy" and "liberty" on "class enemies" and "counterrevolutionary elements" in his own country.

Pyongyang's heated response to developments in Poland further reinforced the doubts about revisionism expressed by Kim at the Fifth Party Congress. It was also a measure of the low state to which relations between the DPRK and the East European countries had fallen since 1968. The events in Czechoslovakia and President Nixon's visit to Bucharest in 1968 did little to allay Pyongyang's doubts about developments in that part of the world. By 1970, Pyongyang was even more inclined to look to the countries in revolutionary ferment in Asia, Africa, and Latin America as areas for DPRK diplomatic initiatives. Increasingly, the Third World augured well for Pyongyang's plan to broaden its base of trade relations and to widen international support for its proposals for the unification of Korea. Little did Pyongyang realize that the circumstances contributing to its renewed confidence belied the presence of more fundamental underlying currents that were already beginning to well up to change the course of North Korea's foreign relations.

THE IMPACT OF THE SINO-AMERICAN DETENTE

The signing of the Shanghai communique on February 27, 1972, between President Richard Nixon and Premier Chou En-lai had a momentous impact on North Korea. The communique, in which both signatories agreed to renounce hegemony in the Asia-Pacific region and to oppose the efforts of any "country or group of countries to establish hegemony," and their stated opposition to collusion between countries "against other countries" and to efforts by major countries "to divide the world into spheres of interest" ended the era of cold war confrontation between Washington and Peking.[14] With two key statements, both sides agreed to undo the basis of suspicion upon which responses were triggered to mutually perceived threats of political and ideological aggrandizement.[15] For the DPRK, the end of China's policy of confrontation against the United States further eroded any hopes for a return to militant confrontation with "imperialism" that may still have been nurtured in Pyongyang.

It was not surprising, therefore, that when the news of the secret meeting between Secretary of State Henry Kissinger and Premier Chou En-lai prior to President Nixon's historic visit to Peking reached Pyongyang, it was greeted in silence. Although it was in keeping with Pyongyang's customary practice to keep news of unwanted developments abroad from the masses, there was undoubtedly some shock within the DPRK. The dramatic news of the turnabout immediately placed Peking in the anomalous position of convincing Pyongyang of the efficacy of dealing with the United States. Unlike the humiliation visited on the Japanese by the "Nixon shock," the response in Pyongyang was orchestrated to emerge with a minimum of "loss of face." The public release of the news of the Nixon visit to Peking was timed to coincide with the state visit of Prince Norodom Sihanouk, whose arrival was billed as that of the "Head of State of Cambodia and Chairman of the National United Front of Kampuchea." Sihanouk's first major state visit out of Peking at least bore the earmarks of the arrival of a friendly Chinese emissary. It also provided Kim Il-song with a notable entry into the world of Third World diplomacy. The arrangements apparently assuaged the pride of Kim Il-song, who responded to the occasion by explaining that:

> Under the historic circumstances in which
> U.S. imperialism had been driven into a blind

alley . . . internally and externally, Nixon made public some time ago his plan to visit China.

This means that the hostile policy towards China which the U.S. imperialists have recklessly pursued for more than 20 years to check by "force" the course of great revolutionary changes in China making up nearly a quarter of the world population has eventually gone to complete bankruptcy and this denotes that the U.S. imperialists have at last succumbed to the pressure of the mighty anti-imperialist revolutionary forces of the world.

In the last analysis, Nixon is going to turn up in Peking with a white flag just as the U.S. imperialist aggressors who suffered defeat in the Korean War in the past came out to Panmunjom with a white flag.[16]

The rapprochement between Washington and Peking capped a series of frustrating developments for Pyongyang. The bloody Sino-Soviet border clashes had already dispelled any illusion that may have yet persisted in Pyongyang about prospects for a revitalized Sino-Soviet alliance. Pyongyang, which had mounted a futile bid for a united front in the Vietnam War, was forced to look on helplessly as the United States, far from falling into a deeper quagmire over the war, moved instead to implement a strategy designed to effect a multipolar balance of power aimed at both Moscow and Peking.[17] A major cornerstone of that strategy was the restoration of U.S.-Chinese relations as a hedge against Moscow's rising power.[18] By preying on Peking's fear of a Soviet military invasion and by simultaneously triggering Soviet alarm over the possibility of U.S.-Chinese collusion, Washington was able to use the Sino-Soviet hostility to its own advantage.[19]

The Sino-American rapprochement was only a prelude to other developments. The Shanghai communique in effect also allowed China to move toward an improvement of relations with Japan. By agreeing to support China's view that Taiwan is part of China, the United States gained an unstated assent to the continuance of U.S.-Taiwan diplomacy and to its right to uphold its mutual defense obligations to Taipei. The unprecedented accord over discords gave China's claim to Taiwan a perceptible psychological boost and the added benefit of U.S. support for Peking's efforts to prevent the resurgence of a dominant Japanese role in Taiwan in the wake of a diminishing American presence. Thus, although the antihegemony clause in the Shanghai communique was primarily an anti-Soviet provision, it also helped to allay Chinese fears of a Japanese threat to its own interests in Taiwan.

Peking's opening to Tokyo was understood to have been offered under the following terms: (1) that the Japan-U.S. Security Treaty and the 1969 Japan-U.S. Joint Communique need not stand in the way of establishing diplomatic relations between Japan and China; (2) that China would waive reparations claims against Japan; (3) that China was desirous of concluding a peace and friendship agreement with Japan that would invalidate the Taiwan-Japan treaty; (4) that China would favorably consider acceptance of export credit facilities such as export-import bank loans if the terms are on an internationally acceptable level; (5) that Peking would favorably consider Japanese participation in oil exploration in China with provisions for crude exports to Japan; and (6) that China would be willing to send specialist missions to Japan for talks on steel, heavy electricals, oil, and agriculture.[20]

The normalization of relations between China and Japan on September 29, 1972, provided further evidence of China's concern over the possibility of a Soviet containment, which was once an accusation reserved for Washington.[21] Japan's recognition of Mongolia soon after the Nixon visit to Peking, Soviet Foreign Minister Gromyko's visit to Tokyo in January, the visit of a high-ranking Soviet trade minister to Tokyo, and signs of impending Soviet-Japanese agreements to develop the oil fields of Siberia stirred fears of a Soviet-Japanese alliance in Peking. A wariness over such an eventuality appears to have compelled Chou to push forward an agreement with the Tanaka government with the understanding that the U.S.-Japan Security Treaty would remain in effect. The provision allowed Prime Minister Tanaka to live up to his commitment to maintain its joint defense alignment with the United States under the American nuclear umbrella as a precondition to a Japanese agreement with the PRC.

The crucial agreements reached by the PRC with the United States and Japan in 1972 undercut the narrow anti-American and anti-Japanese premise upon which PRC-DPRK relations were restored in 1970 during Chou En-lai's visit to Pyongyang.[22] Clearly, a new framework of relations had begun to evolve in the Asia-Pacific area with China gaining recognition as a great power by the United States and Japan. It was a hopeful step toward a new regional accommodation where national interests and spheres of influence would be allowed to emerge beyond the narrow constraints of conflicting ideologies and where accidental nuclear exchanges could be averted among the great powers. Such a dramatic turnabout would have been impossible without China's own recognition of its own vulnerability to the "bear at the gate."[23] Pyongyang and Seoul, for their part, had no choice but to accede to reality lest the destiny of Korea be determined by "outsiders."

Once the major powers had agreed on ways to disagree, the way was left open for the Koreans themselves to approach each other, not as apologists for incompatible political and ideological systems but as Koreans.

NORTH-SOUTH CONTACTS AND THE UNIFICATION ISSUE

Tentative steps toward a constructive dialogue between North and South representatives began during the period of the "ping-pong diplomacy." At that time, talks were opened between the Red Cross Societies of North and South Korea to discuss contacts between relatives on both sides.

The most dramatic response to the new international situation, however, occurred on May 2, 1972, when Lee Hu-rak, Director of the ROK Central Intelligence Agency, crossed over from Panmunjom to Kaesong before boarding a specially dispatched North Korean helicopter to Pyongyang for four days of lengthy discussions with Kim Il-song and his brother Kim Yong-chu, Director of the Organization and Guidance Department of the KWP. From May 29 to June 1, 1972, North Korean Vice-Premier Pak Song-ch'ol paid a reciprocal visit to Seoul, also in secrecy, to confer with President Pak Chong-hui and other South Korean officials.

On July 4, 1972, a joint communique was simultaneously released by Seoul and Pyongyang containing an agreement on seven points designed to ease tensions in the Korean peninsula and to bring about the eventual reunification of Korea. The communique also stipulated that by "peaceful means" a "great national unity shall be sought above all transcending differences in ideas, ideologies and systems." At the same time, both sides pledged to refrain from propaganda mudslinging and "take positive measures to prevent inadvertent military incidents."[24]

However, it soon became evident that it was easier to achieve a consensus on the external threat than on the internal threat to Korean reunification. The 27 years of habituation to conflicting ideologies and vastly disparate life-styles had obviously taken their toll on both sides. The blatant propaganda statements of the Northern delegates to the Red Cross talks carried live on television in Seoul offended the Seoulites, who, in spite of their own conflicts with governmental autocracy, had come to regard political dissidence as a natural part of their existence. Moreover, journalists from Seoul who abhorred autocracy at home found the autocracy in Pyongyang even more revolting.[25] On the other hand, the Northern delegates to Seoul found the bourgeois life-style reflected in such things as scantily clad nightclub stage performers and miniskirted girls in the streets far too dangerous to contemplate for the life-style of the severely regimented northerners.

At the leadership level, although Pak Chong-hui and Kim Il-song had come to the realization that detente between the United States, the USSR, and the PRC was inexorable, both were determined to confront each other from a position of strength. For President Pak, who had come into office of the strength of his ability to stand up to the threat of the North, the first move was to proclaim martial law on October 17, 1972. In the face of rising domestic opposition and increasing criticism of his authoritarianism in the West, ironically, it was Kim Il-song who furnished Pak with the rationale that he needed to strengthen his hand in Seoul. On November 27, 1972, the Pak government scrapped the old constitution and adopted a new constitution that virtually suspended many of the democratic rights that were provided by the previous constitution. Apparently, Pak felt far more secure facing up to Kim Il-song's rigidly regimented and indoctrinated country with virtual dictatorial powers.

On December 27, 1972, Kim Il-song countered by presiding over the adoption of a new constitution in the North. The intent was the same on both sides as each sought to forge more efficient systems of political rule over their countries. However, there was obviously less need for change in the Northern constitution. The pragmatic intent of the new DPRK constitution was reflected in its greater emphasis on centralized controls over the economy and on its enhancement as "a sharp weapon of the dictatorship of the proletariat" with tighter links between party and government roles.

In short, the talks between the North and the South have led to what Gregory Henderson has characterized as "essentially ones between two dictatorships with political systems that, while certainly different, are now far closer in structure and concentration of power than before."[26]

By early 1973, hopes for an improvement in North-South relations began to fade as a new propaganda offensive began to materialize in the North against the South. In June 1973, clandestine broadcasts against the South were resumed and the exacerbation in North-South relations culminated in the suspension of talks over the Kim Tae-chung incident. The forcible abduction of Kim Tae-chung from a hotel room in Tokyo and his subsequent appearance in Seoul allowed the North to suspend the talks by blaming Lee Hu-rak, Director of the ROK Central Intelligence Agency, who was also the top Southern representative in the North-South talks. The resultant flareup in relations between Tokyo and Seoul also played into the hands of Pyongyang. Although Pyongyang's level of economic involvement with Japan was also rising remarkably, it is said that North Korea's main concern was to prevent an increasing Japanese penetration into South Korea since, in Pyongyang's view, a greater Japanese economic involvement in South Korea would inevitably involve a greater Japanese military involvement at a later stage.[27]

    Meanwhile, with the onset of detente, Pyongyang began to identify increasingly with the Third World. In 1972, the DPRK opened diplomatic relations with Uganda, Cameroon, Madagascar, Upper Volta, Zaire, and Pakistan. In 1973, Afghanistan, Bangladesh, India, Liberia, Mauritius, Togo, Dahomey, Denmark, Finland, Iceland, Norway, Sweden, and Argentina were added. To dramatize its support for the cause of the Third World countries, North Korea also dispatched pilots to fly "defensive" missions in Egypt and Syria during the Arab-Israeli conflict of 1973. North Korea also took particular delight over the hardship brought on the United States and the industrialized countries of the West by the oil embargo of late 1973. Pyongyang was also well aware of the effects of the oil embargo on Seoul and in late 1973 and early 1974 began to take advantage of the lull in North-South talks by engaging in a series of violations of the Northern Patrol Limitation Line, claiming the territorial rights to five islets in the Western Sea that had been ceded to South Korea under the terms of the Armistice Agreement.[28] The provocations were probably designed to test the U.S. will to respond to such acts and to remind the South of the North's determination to pursue unification through militant means.

    The broadbased international effort by the DPRK was designed to enhance Pyongyang's image overseas at the expense of Seoul and, ultimately, to isolate the ROK. From Pyongyang's vantage point, the most promising avenue to sympathy and eventual recognition was the Third World.

THE REALITIES OF COEXISTENCE

    For over two decades, a pro forma ritual governed the Korean question at the UN. Each year, Pyongyang's unwillingness to recognize the competence of the UN would disallow its presence at the deliberations. It always remained for the South Korean delegate to present the ROK's position, at the end of which the debate would be deferred for another year.

    In May 1973, North Korea's quiet admission to the World Health Organization suddenly conferred on it an official observer status at the UN, thereby ending its longstanding isolation from UN deliberations. With the aid of the Chinese delegation, Pyongyang immediately sought a proposal that would dissolve the UN Commission for the Unification and Rehabilitation of Korea and with it the withdrawal of the UN "cover" designation from the U.S. forces stationed in South Korea. With that, Pyongyang hoped to end the UN legitimization for the American military presence as a first step toward the eventual removal of the U.S. forces from the Korean peninsula. The Chinese-sponsored proposal marked a point of departure from previous Soviet-sponsored proposals that relied on hostile rhetoric and direct calls for the withdrawal of U.S. troops from South Korea, which inevitably triggered U.S. opposition.

The pro-North resolution, which was opposed by a pro-South resolution calling for the simultaneous UN entry of both Koreas, failed to muster the required support and was shelved by its Algerian sponsor. But North Korea's unremitting diplomatic offensive carried into 1974 with the brunt of the offensive still concentrated on the withdrawal of "foreign troops" from Korean soil. The Nixon Doctrine in 1969 and "Vietnamization" in 1971 indicating U.S. discouragement over further involvement in land warfare on the Asian continent, made the United States a likely target in Pyongyang's strategy of attrition, especially in view of the unyielding posture of the Pak government. The removal of the U.S. forces in South Korea would not only diminish the chances for an immediate U.S. retaliation in response to a Northern invation but the Koreanization of the Korean question would also reduce the chances of a big power clash in the Korean peninsula. Pyongyang seemed confident that once the confrontation was reduced to the two Koreas, the overall strength of the North would prevail.

The other leg in Pyongyang's strategy was to do away with the 1953 armistice agreement since the only other signatory to the agreement besides North Korea and China was the UN Command. Any new arrangement to replace the UN Command with a "suitable and workable arrangement" as proposed by the South would have to include South Korea as a signatory--an arrangement that the North would be unwilling to accept since it would result in a recognition of the South or a divided Korea. Kim Il-song's own opinion on the matter was that it was "an internal affair of the Koreans themselves" that no "third party should meddle in."[29] Pyongyang's answer to the problem was a creation of a North-South Military Commission to replace the Korean armistice agreement, which would also enhance Pyongyang's chances of isolating Seoul.[30] The measure of Pyongyang's diplomatic success in 1974 was to be seen in the slim one-vote margin by which the resolution in support of the North Korea proposal to end the UN presence in Korea and withdraw all U.S. forces failed in the General Assembly.

The failure of the pro-North resolution in the General Assembly in 1974 was also attributable to a lack of overriding support for the resolution from Moscow and Peking.[31] Moscow had long grown weary of Kim Il-song's transparent efforts to keep Moscow at arms length while it moved in support of Peking. On the other hand, there was little inclination by the Chinese to see U.S. troops being withdrawn from either South Korea or Japan in view of the Soviet menace. Moreover, both Moscow and Peking were well aware of the U.S. determination to use its veto power within the Security Council to preserve the existing military arrangements in the South.

Peking's involvement in Pyongyang's affairs throughout the 1970s was complicated by Kim Il-song's sensitivity at being an accessory for Peking's strategy to keep Moscow at bay in Asia. But from Peking's standpoint, the strategy of keeping Pyongyang in tow was one way of denying Soviet hegemony in the Korean peninsula. The Pyongyang connection also provided Peking with a useful position from which to caution the North against another invasion of the South that could conceivably involve the Chinese in another war with the United States. Moreover, a clash with the United States would also have raised the immediate threat of a Soviet invasion along its own border areas. Under those circumstances, even Japan would have to consider rearming.

It was to Peking's advantage to convince Pyongyang of the advantage of adopting a diplomatic strategy paralleling Peking's approach to the Taiwan issue. The American pledge in the Shanghai communique to withdraw its troops from Taiwan "as the tension in the area diminishes" was sufficient cause for Peking not only to lessen tensions in the surrounding areas but also to diminish any tension that may detract from its diplomatic strategy. By going along with Peking, Pyongyang has benefited from Chinese support among the nonaligned nations and at least pro forma support within the UN General Assembly.

Also, Peking's preference for a two-Koreas arrangement at least for the present has produced a useful trade-off for both sides. The continuing American presence has at least forestalled a dominant Japanese influence in Korea and the Sino-American rapprochement has allowed Peking to move ahead with its efforts to improve its relationship with Tokyo. Peking seems to have convinced Pyongyang that this also was the proper course for Pyongyang to take since even a policy of "equidistant relations" by Tokyo vis-a-vis the two Koreas would detract heavily from Seoul's present one-sided relationship with Tokyo.[32]

Peking's determination to keep Kim Il-song on the diplomatic track was particularly evident during the period of uncertainty that followed the downfall of Saigon to Communist forces in the spring of

1975. On April 12, 1975, the day of Kim's sixty-third birthday, it was suddenly announced that Kim Il-song would pay an official visit to the PRC. The huge public welcome accorded Kim upon his arrival in Peking indicated Peking's desire to reassure Kim of its continuing support.

Although the possibility of a North Korean probe may have been discussed in private, it was obvious that the Chinese were unwilling to even consider such a risk. As noted in the Sino-Korean communique, a more feasible course was for the DPRK to strengthen their ties "with the people of all countries, particularly the Third World countries." It also added that:

> More and more countries in the world have established diplomatic relations with the Democratic People's Republic of Korea. As the sole sovereign state of the Korean nation, the Democratic People's Republic of Korea is enjoying an even higher international prestige and playing an even greater role in international affairs.[33]

Peking's first public reference to Pyongyang as the "sole sovereign state" in Korea indicated that while Kim may have agreed not to stand in the way of detente for now, he may have felt that he had the right to insist on preferential treatment and greater support from Peking on the two-Koreas issues and on the issue of the U.S. withdrawal of troops from South Korea. Peking, for its part, blamed "U.S. imperialism for pursuing a policy of two Koreas"; it called for the dissolution of the UN Command and for the withdrawal of U.S. forces from Korea without ever mentioning when they should take place.[34]

Peking also went out of its way to dampen "foreign" speculation about a possible North Korean invasion of the South with Chinese backing by pointing to dissidence within South Korea as the real revolutionary threat to the South. Peking noted that Kim's announced intention to refrain from standing idly by in the event of a revolution in the South was a "natural and logical" response to a revolutionary condition that could only be presumed to be at the instigation of the South Koreans themselves.[35]

However, it should also be noted that whereas Teng Hsiao-ping referred to the "scramble between the superpowers for world hegemony," which is "becoming more and more fierce," Kim very discreetly avoided any mention of the superpowers or hegemony when it was his turn to speak on the occasion. Kim's response and show of "independence," at least to the extent of refusing to openly support Peking's attack on the Soviet Union, was certain to have been monitored by the Kremlin.

At the same time, by reacting quickly to force the return of the Mayaguez, a ship captured by Cambodian forces soon after the fall of Saigon, and by making it clear that the United States was determined to use even tactical nuclear weapons to defend South Korea, Washington also made it clear to Pyongyang that it was well advised to refrain from provoking the South.

The policy of moderation apparently agreed on between Peking and Pyongyang was soon manifested within weeks of the Peking visit by Kim. In May, Kim Il-song embarked on a diplomatic mission that took him through Rumania, Algeria, Mauritania, Bulgaria, and Yugoslavia. The trip served two purposes. First, it allowed Kim to reassure the outside world of his commitment to the "peaceful unification" of Korea, and second, it allowed him to put his personal weight behind North Korea's efforts to gain entry into the nonaligned bloc and to present a personal appeal for the adoption of a pro-Pyongyang resolution in the UN General Assembly. North Korea's identity with the Third World was given prominence in every country except Bulgaria.[36]

Kim's cautiousness was particularly evident in Bucharest, where there was no reiteration of a previous North Korean-Rumanian joint statement that there is "no international center" governing relations within the Communist bloc.[37] However, at a ceremony to observe the signing of a treaty of friendship and cooperation between the DPRK and Rumania, Kim remarked that "If we had not invariably maintained the independent principle but acted under any baton, we would not have reached the adoption of such a fine document," indicating that there was still agreement on both sides on the issue of "independence."[38] That statement, plus the agreement between the two sides to defend their "sovereignty and interests," especially after Peking had, for the first time, referred to the DPRK's "sovereignty" a few weeks prior to that, provided tacit North Korean support for Rumania's standing opposition to the Brezhnev Doctrine.[39] The developments in Bucharest may have added to the reasons behind the Kremlin's refusal to invite Kim Il-song to Moscow during 1975.

The efficacy of the diplomatic course charted by Pyongyang with Chinese support was borne out on August 26, 1974, when North Korea was admitted to the nonaligned bloc along with North Vietnam and the Palestinian Liberation Organization.[40] The event immediately raised the prospect of a favorable vote for the North Korean resolution at the 1975 UN General Assembly deliberations on the Korean question.

However, on November 18, 1975, an unprecedented development occurred at the UN. The General Assembly voted to adopt two contradictory resolutions on the Korean question. The Assembly adopted a pro-South resolution that called for the dissolution of the

UN Command by the end of the year, with the proviso that Pyongyang would agree to an acceptable alternative to the armistice. Under the resolution, the dissolution of the UN Command would invalidate the armistice agreement of 1953, which was signed by North Korea, China, and the UN Command. The pro-North resolution adopted by the Assembly called for the withdrawal from South Korea of all foreign troops operating under the UN flag and for the conclusion of a peace treaty between "the real parties concerned," meaning the United States and the DPRK, and not the ROK.[41]

North Korea greeted its entry into the UN as a victory. However, although Pyongyang has recently met with success in the conduct of its foreign relations, it has not been without cost. By adhering closely to Peking's line, it has alienated the Kremlin, and its headlong drive to gain technological parity with Seoul has saddled it with sizable foreign debts and credit problems abroad at a time of worldwide economic ills.[42]

Abroad, the extravagant claims for the thought of Kim Il-song have fallen on cynicism, and in spite of the bold front and the highly promethean spirit that animates its policies, Pyongyang must still find some way to free itself from the fetters of great power interests and to accommodate itself to the realities of a national life that will continue to flow along causeways that cannot be altered even by its vaunted Sun of the Nation.[43]

NOTES

1. Chou might have also reminded Pyongyang of the presence of Russian units along Korean borders. According to a Japanese source, eight Soviet armored divisions deployed from the Ussuri River area to the southern coastal areas of Lake Baikal and all the way to the DPRK borders would probably have provided the breakthroughs for an invasion of China. Gendai Chugoku (Contemporary China), Tokyo, no. 8 (December 1973), p. 102.

2. Criticisms on economic planning were not limited to Peking. In a major theoretical discussion entitled "On Some Theoretical Problems of Socialist Economy," Kim Il-song criticized both "right and left opportunists" for causing confusion and harm in the practical struggle for Socialist and Communist construction. Pyongyang Times, March 17, 1969.

3. Kankoku-Hoku Chosen Jimmei Jiten (Biographical Dictionary of South and North Korea). Sekei Seikei Chosakaihan (Compilations of the Research Association for World Political Economies) (Tokyo, 1973), p. 92.

4. Pyongyang Times, April 13, 1970.

5. Ibid.

6. The hijacked Japan Airlines plane landed in Pyongyang on April 3, 1970 and was allowed to depart on April 5, 1970. Pyongyang Times, April 6, 1970.

7. Korean Central News Agency, Korean Central Yearbook, 1971, p. 579.

8. North Korea's economic development was highly dependent on the Soviet Union from 1945-56; it adopted an independent posture from 1957-60; it became dependent on China as relations with the Soviet Union worsened from 1961-65; it became dependent on the Soviet Union as relations with China worsened from 1966-70; it became dependent on China from 1970-71; and a policy of equidistant relations was adopted beginning in 1972. Tongso Munje Yonguso (Research Center of East-West Problems), Pukhan Kyongje (The Economics of North Korea) (Seoul: Chungang Ilbo, 1973), p. 27.

9. From 1948 to 1970, 53 percent of all aid to the DPRK came from the Soviet Union, 30 percent from the PRC, and 17 percent from the East European countries. Of the East European countries, East Germany contributed 8 percent, Poland 5.3 percent, and Rumania 3.7 percent. Ibid., p. 28.

10. Pyongyang Times, August 29, 1968.

11. The full membership of the Political Committee formed at the Fifth Party Congress consisted of: Kim Il-song, Ch'oe Yong-kon, Kim Il, Pak Song-ch'ol, Ch'oe Hyon, Kim Yong-chu, O Chin-u, Kim Tong-kyu, So Ch'ol, Kim Chung-nin, Han Ik-su. The candidate members were: Hyon Mu-kwang, Chong Ch'un-t'aek, Yang Hyong-sop, and Kim Man-kum. Nodong Sinmun, November 14, 1970.

12. Robert A. Scalapino and Chong-Sik Lee, Communism in Korea, 2 vols. (Berkeley: University of California Press, 1972), pp. 747-48.

13. Nodong Sinmun, February 4, 1971.

14. Akira Iriye, The Cold War in Asia: A Historical Introduction (Englewood Cliffs, N.J.: Prentice-Hall, 1974), pp. 1-2.

15. Professor Iriye notes that, "The United States through its responses of 1950 (the Korean War) made it clear that it would redefine the structure of Asian-Pacific international relations on the basis of three principles: the revitalization of Japan once again as a power, the extension of American power in Southeast Asia, and the detachment of Taiwan from mainland China." Ibid., p. 181.

16. Pyongyang Times, August 14, 1971.

17. Edith Lenart, "How Peace Became Desirable," Far Eastern Economic Review 78, no. 45 (November 4, 1972): 12.

18. William E. Griffith, The Washington Papers: Peking, Moscow and Beyond (Beverly Hills, Calif.: Sage, 1973), p. 4.

19. Ibid., p. 5.

20. Koji Nakamura, "Open Door for China," Far Eastern Economic Review, September 2, 1972, p. 13.

21. It has been speculated when Kissinger went to Peking in 1971 he carried with him satellite pictures of the Soviet military buildup on China's northern frontiers. The resultant view was that U.S. spying may not be as damnable as Soviet spying. Derek Davies, "Traveler's Tales," Far Eastern Economic Review 89, no. 31 (August 1, 1975): 17.

22. Kim Il-song may have discussed the PRC's agreement with Japan during an unpublicized and unannounced trip to Peking in October 1972. In an interview with Japanese Diet member Tokuma Utsunomiya, Kim revealed that he made a trip to Peking to help Norodom Sihanouk observe his fiftieth birthday. Sihanouk's birthday is listed as October 31, 1922. Yomiuri Shinbun, August 19, 1975.

23. Harold C. Hinton, The Bear at the Gate: Chinese Policy-Making Under Soviet Pressure (American Enterprise Institute and Stanford, Calif.: Hoover Institution, 1971).

24. Washington Post, July 4, 1972. For the three principles of reunification see, Pyongyang Times, July 6, 1972.

25. W. E. Skillend, "Korea Today," Asian Affairs (Journal of the Royal Central Asian Society) 62, pt. 1 (new series vol. 6): 18-19.

26. Gregory Henderson, Richard Lebow, John Stoessinger, Divided Nations in a Divided World (New York: David McKay Co., 1974), p. 86.

27. Young C. Kim, "North Korea's Reunification Policy: A Magnificent Obsession?" Journal of Korean Affairs 3, no. 4 (January 1974): 16-17.

28. Lee Ki-taek, "North Korean Military Policy Toward South Korea," East Asian Review 1, no. 2 (Summer 1974): 147.

29. Speech by Kim Il-song to welcome President Asad of Syria. Nodong Sinmun, October 2, 1974.

30. Foreign policy speech by Foreign Minister Ho Tam. Nodong Sinmun, November 9, 1974.

31. Although North Korea's UN observers made much of the nonaligned countries' resolution in support of North Korea at the summit conference held just prior to the UN debate on the Korean question, unmentioned was the fact that the pro-Pyongyang resolution was submitted by its supporters on the last day and in the middle of the night when no dissent was possible. Louis Halasz, "The Victory March," Far Eastern Economic Review 82, no. 47 (November 26, 1973): 22.

32. North Korea's denunciation of Japan began to abate soon after the Sino-Japan rapprochement. Kim Il-song is reported to have

said to Tokuma Utsunomiya that "It is not good for visitors to leave this country with bad impressions. Japanese visitors are not displeased when they visit here now, as there are no longer any slogans opposing Japanese militarism. Such slogans might be found in museums but they are not taught in school any longer." Yomiuri Shinbun, August 19, 1975.

33. "Joint Communique of the People's Republic of China and the Democratic People's Republic of Korea," Peking Review, no. 18 (May 2, 1975): p. 9.

34. Ibid.

35. "Chung Ch'ao kung pao ho ch'ao hsien pan tao hsing shih" (The Sino-Korean Communique and the Situation in the Korean Peninsula), Hong Kong, Ta Kung-pao, April 19, 1975, p. 2. There were also reports of official and unofficial assurances from Peking that the Chinese would not back North Korea in any military adventure. Dana Adams Schmidt, "Does U.S. Defend Park Too Strongly?" The Christian Science Monitor, July 14, 1975.

36. See, U.S. Joint Publications Research Service, Translations on North Korea (Kim Il-song's Tour of Eastern Europe and North Africa), no. 413, JPRS 65101 (June 27, 1975).

37. See, the joint communique on the visit of Nicolae Ceausescu to the DPRK in Pyongyang Times, June 19, 1971.

38. Translations on North Korea, op. cit., no. 413, p. 10.

39. The joint communique also recognized "the importance of achieving European security," an obviously pro-Chinese view. Pyongyang Times, June 7, 1975.

40. The nonaligned summit was attended by delegates from 80 developing countries from Asia, Africa, and Latin America, plus Yugoslavia and Malta from Europe. The New York Times, August 27, 1975, p. 9.

41. The pro-South resolution passed by a vote of 59 to 51 with 29 abstentions. The pro-North resolution passed by a vote of 61 to 43 with 32 abstentions. The North Korean Party organ responded to the event by acknowledging the passage of only the pro-Pyongyang resolution. It did not report the passage of the pro-South resolution. Nodong Sinmun, November 20, 1975.

42. Estimates are that the DPRK owes anywhere from $200 million to $500 million in the West and as much as $750 million within the Communist bloc. See, Washington Post, March 13, 1975; Susumu Awanohara, "North Korea: Deeper in Debt," Far Eastern Economic Review 88, no. 23 (June 6, 1975): 52; and Fowler Martin, "Pyongyang: Shedding Light on Deficits," Far Eastern Economic Review, August 1, 1975, p. 49.

43. A French source reported that, "The DPRK recently made a shattering entry into the French press. For three days

straight, entire pages of <u>France-Soir</u>, purchased by the North Korean government answered questions which, in all truthfulness we are not asking, without providing the answer to the sole question which continues to intrigue us--why? . . . It is hard to imagine by what perversion of spirit the responsible functionaries thought they could, by paying for it, interest public opinion in the Western countries in a year-old speech devoted strictly to local problems, written in the style of a licensed translator, to tell the world, 'We must energetically promote the work to enlarge the Musan mine. . . .'"
<u>L'Express</u>, Paris, April 28-May 4, 1975, p. 81.

CHAPTER 7
CONCLUSION

Predatory foreign aggression and a veiled uneasiness over the implications of domestic incohesiveness in light of such threats are underlying features of North Korea's foreign relations. They are legacies of a tradition of submission to great power politics and domestic factionalism that has historically beset Korea. Today, the massive outpouring of public adulation for Kim Il-song, who stands as the living symbol of national resolve and resistance to external challenges; the incessant hate campaigns waged against "internal and external" enemies; and the frenetic pace of production campaigns aimed at self-reliance are symptomatic of those traditional concerns. Pyongyang's own references to Kim Il-song as the first national savior to appear in 5,000 years of Korean history in itself attests to the void that has existed in its own tradition of nationalism. Yet, "old ideological remnants" die hard and until North Korean nationalism is blessed with mass spontaneity, Kim Il-song is convinced of his indispensability as the rallying point of national loyalty. By raising the traditional threat of flunkeyism, Kim has been able to justify his elimination of factionalists who have dared to look to foreign countries for support, and he has skillfully manipulated the threat of the great powers to Korea to heighten internal vigilance against dissidents and to deflect domestic tensions so that they are directed against real or imagined threats from the outside world.

As the dominant figure who has towered over North Korean politics for the past 30 years, it is impossible to discount Kim Il-song's role in Pyongyang's foreign relations. Kim's role and his problems are unique because of the peculiar circumstances that initially dictated the role that he was to play in North Korea. Whereas the revolution in China was aided considerably by Maoist solutions to China's problems in North Korea, Stalinist solutions worked because

CONCLUSION

it was the Russians and not the Koreans who marched into Pyongyang as "liberators" at the end of World War II.

Yet, even under the most favorable circumstances, neither the charity of a powerful overbearing nation nor its chosen overlords can provide the most desirable basis upon which to embark on a program of national reconstruction. In North Korea, policy was hampered by cold war considerations that gave Soviet "advice" an eminently militant cast. A fear of U.S. imperialist incursions into North Korea was as much the goad to action as the moral imperatives of proletarian internationalism. Kim Il-song was merely a part of the overall Soviet plan for what would now be regarded by Peking as Soviet hegemony.

Once the entry of the Chinese People's Volunteers into the Korean War began to undermine the dominant Soviet influence in North Korea, it was only a matter of time before Pyongyang's desire for greater independence would be allowed to assert itself. The outbreak of the Sino-Soviet dispute increased Pyongyang's opportunity to pursue a more independent course in its relations with other countries.

As Kim's level of independence increased, he also found it progressively necessary to bolster his political legitimacy as well as his power base. Ironically, like his Japanese colonial predecessors, Kim himself was initially devoid of roots in the Korean political culture. Long years abroad and the presence of more experienced and established political competitors made it necessary for Kim to seek a more viable political image to sustain his legitimacy as a leader. Throughout the years, Kim has proven his skill as a political infighter, but at every step of the way he has had to bolster and refine a self-image suitable to his perceived station in life. He began by ridding himself of the image of being a Soviet or Chinese pawn and turned instead to his Korean heritage.

Kim Il-song has shown himself to be a bold manipulator of men and events in setting himself up as the sole beneficiary of national political allegiance in the DPRK. He has learned to rely on mass line techniques to forge controls that extend down to every sector of the country. By relying on the masses and by making a credible attempt to make them feel that they themselves have had a hand in the decision-making process, Kim has been able to mobilize a new national consciousness and also avoid the wrath of mass discontent. In a sense, Kim has practiced a form of bureaucratic despotism in which administrative ploys have been skillfully employed to exploit labor through an unremitting series of production campaigns. Major national achievements became ready sources of national pride and Kim himself has been the most notable beneficiary of those achievements.

However, throughout three decades, the foremost goal in the foreign relations of the DPRK, the reunification of Korea, has eluded

Kim Il-song. In the 1950s, Pyongyang resorted to war to take over the South and failed. In the 1960s, it employed paramilitary tactics and subversion to undermine Seoul and that too failed. In the 1970s, Pyongyang has largely concentrated on diplomacy to isolate the South. Yet in spite of growing Third World recognition, Pyongyang still remains deterred by great power interests. Detente among the great powers has led to a crumbling of alliances based on ideology, forcing North and South Korea to seek their own solutions to unification.

Thus, after 30 years, Pyongyang finds itself still deterred from its foremost objective by (1) detente, which it opposes but is powerless to obstruct; (2) disunity within the Socialist camp, especially between Moscow and Peking, without whose continuing support there can be no hope of sustaining large-scale warfare against the South; (3) the presence of U.S. military forces in the South backed by Washington's expressed willingness to use tactical nuclear weapons on Northern forces in the event of an all-out invasion of the ROK; and (4) the presence of a battle-tested ROK army and a citizenry with little inclination to succumb willingly to Northern propaganda blandishments in the South.

The elusiveness of reunification cannot be attributed solely to external circumstances. Pyongyang's policy initiatives must also be held accountable. Kim traded opportunistically on the conflict between Moscow and Peking to consolidate his own domestic stronghold and also to become a broker for North Korean and small-country interests. In that quest, Pyongyang's major undoing was not at the hands of Moscow, Peking, or Washington. Pyongyang was undermined as much by its own strategy of relying on terrorism and subversion. The activities of North Korean trained terrorists in areas like Latin America, as well as the <u>Pueblo</u> and EC-121 incidents, alarmed the Socialist countries as much as many of the other countries. More recently, its international debts have begun to hurt the credit ratings of other countries of the bloc seeking financial aid from the capitalistic nations.

Moreover, by exporting advice and training in terrorism and subversion in the 1960s, it abrogated a fundamental tenet of chuche by infringing on the independence and sovereignty of other countries. Such tactics tended to expose the limits of Kim's vision and perception abroad. At times, Pyongyang seemed to be completely oblivious to the fact that its lease on international life was largely guaranteed by mutual security arrangements with both Moscow and Peking. However, once Pyongyang began to tout the sagacity of Kim Il-song's views with bold assassination plots against Seoul and deliberate acts of provocations against the United States to back its boastful assertions, there was cause for alarm in all the major capitals of the great powers. The alarm was particularly evident in Moscow and Peking

CONCLUSION

where the "defense" of the DPRK was not taken to include the encouragement of North Korean "offensives."

Instead of dramatizing the need for a united front against the United States and forcing Moscow and Peking to end their feud, Pyongyang helped to accelerate the trend toward detente among the great powers. Pyongyang was made to realize that the solidarity that once characterized the Moscow-Peking-Pyongyang axis was even more suspect. At the same time, it was reconfirmed that there were no great ground swells of support for the cult of Kim Il-song in either Moscow or Peking. The Kremlin's contempt for Kim's brashness and for his recent tilt toward Peking has eroded Soviet support for the DPRK. At the same time, China's interest in maintaining a U.S. military presence in Asia as a hedge against Soviet hegemonism has made Chinese support for Kim Il-song's action programs conditional.

Moreover, in this era of detente, Kim realizes that a mistake in his manipulation of the Sino-Soviet dispute can be costly to his own quest for unification. The problem now is that ever since the Shanghai communique of 1972, Pyongyang's own balancing act has been overshadowed by an American balancing act between Moscow and Peking. Kim realizes, for example, that a recognition of the ROK by either Moscow or Peking could undermine his efforts to isolate South Korea internationally. Such a development could also place a freeze on the North-South demarcation. Therefore, while Pyongyang has sought to isolate the ROK by proposing an armistice agreement solely with the United States and to the exclusion of Seoul on the grounds that the United States is the "real power" in the South and that the 1953 armistice did not include the ROK as a signatory, it cannot discount the possibility of moves by Moscow and Peking to improve relations with Seoul, however unlikely that may seem at present. Peking has held the line on this matter but Moscow has allowed individual South Koreans as well as at least one ROK delegation to enter the Soviet Union on UN-related matters. Although Moscow has been able to justify its actions on grounds other than an anti-Pyongyang bias, the implications are clear that the ploy is available, should Moscow ever find the need to pressure the Kim Il-song regime. The United States is aware that it can hold to the position of making a recognition of the DPRK contingent on a recognition of the ROK by Moscow and Peking. But, at the same time, Pyongyang realizes that a four-power solution to the situation in Korea can be forestalled as long as Moscow and Peking are at odds with each other.

Kim Il-song's efforts to reunify Korea on his own terms over the past three decades culminated in the UN General Assembly vote on the Korean question in November 1975. The adoption of the two conflicting resolutions on Korea in effect mirrored the futility of trying to find a solution to a problem over which even world representatives remain divided. The "victory" heralded in Pyongyang over the acceptance of the first pro-Pyongyang resolution by the UN General Assembly succeeded in masking their misgivings about the passage of an accompanying pro-Seoul resolution but it failed to alter the circumstances of the North-South split. In fact, by forcing the issue on the abolishment of the UN Command in South Korea, North Korea may have inadvertently hurt its own cause for unification. It has now made the U.S. presence in South Korea entirely contingent on a bilateral security agreement between Washington and Seoul. More significantly, it has now taken the issue of the U.S. military presence in South Korea out of the UN forum, where North Korea stood to profit from the anti-American sentiments of some of its most vocal supporters. Future attempts by Kim Il-song to call for the forcible removal of U.S. troops from South Korea will therefore have to be made at the risk of denying the right of all sovereign nations to enter into bilateral defense agreements with other nations, including North Korea's own agreements with Moscow and Peking.

As Kim Il-song looks beyond the first 30 years of the DPRK, it is probably with the realization that rapid shifts in the basic premises underlying North Korea's foreign policy options will make his problem of remaining a symbol of success within his own country increasingly difficult. Kim has burnished his personal cult on the presumption that the country has long been in want of a heroic leader. If history is to be the judge of such a presumption, Kim was probably right. The country did need a leader to raise it out of the doldrums of a colonialist past and to overcome the countercurrents of domestic factionalists, many of whom were only too willing to be abetted by foreign assistance. That a national leader given less to the megalomania of Kim could have done just as well or better can be argued, but it is a moot point. In reality, North Korea has known no other leader.

In the international arena, however, like other mortal leaders of the world, it has been part of Kim Il-song's lot to accommodate himself to the forces that have constantly impinged on him and his country, and not to shape them at will. In the process, the forces of change have had a way of exposing the incongruity between his chosen image of omnipotence and his limited purchase over the forces that will always remain beyond his or any nation's control.

SELECTED BIBLIOGRAPHY

Books: English Sources

Acheson, Dean. *Present at the Creation*. New York: W. W. Norton, 1969.

Avineri, Shlomo. *The Social and Political Thought of Karl Marx*. London: Cambridge University Press, 1971.

_____, ed. *Karl Marx on Colonialism and Modernization*. Garden City, N.Y.: Doubleday, 1968.

Baldwin, Frank, ed. *Without Parallel*. New York: Pantheon Books, 1974.

Bohlen, Charles E. *Witness to History 1929-1969*. New York: W. W. Norton, 1973.

Bong, Baik. *Kim Il-song Biography II*. Tokyo: Miraisha, 1970.

Clyde, Paul Hibbert. *The Far East*. New York: Prentice-Hall, 1952.

Cooper, Chester L. *The Lost Crusade: America in Vietnam*. New York: Dodd, Mead, 1970.

Democratic People's Republic of Korea, Academy of Sciences, Research Institute of History. *History of the Just Fatherland Liberation War of the Korean People*. Pyongyang: Foreign Languages Publishing House, 1961.

Democratic People's Republic of Korea. Pyongyang: Foreign Languages Publishing House, 1958.

Dupre, Louis. *The Philosophical Foundations of Marxism*. New York: Harcourt, Brace and World, 1966.

Fairbank, John K. *Trade and Diplomacy on the China Coast: The Opening of the Treaty Ports 1842-1854*. Palo Alto, Calif.: Stanford University Press, 1969.

_____, ed. The Chinese World Order: Traditional China's Foreign Relations. Cambridge, Mass.: Harvard University Press, 1968.

Griffith, William E. The Washington Papers: Peking, Moscow, and Beyond. Beverly Hills, Calif.: Sage, 1973.

Hahm Pyong-choon. The Korean Political Tradition and Law. Seoul: Hollym Corporation Publishers, 1967.

Han, Woo-keun. The History of Korea. Seoul: Eul-Yoo Publishing Co., 1970.

Hatada, Takashi. A History of Korea. Trans. and ed. by Warren W. Smith and Benjamin H. Hazard. Santa Barbara, Calif.: Clio Press, 1969.

Henderson, Gregory, Richard Lebow, and John Stoessinger. Divided Nations in a Divided World. New York: David McKay Co., 1974.

Hinton, Harold C. The Bear at the Gate: Chinese Policy-Making Under Soviet Pressure. American Enterprise Institute and Stanford, Calif.: Hoover Institution, 1971.

_____. China's Turbulent Quest: An Analysis of China's Foreign Relations Since 1945. New York: Macmillan, 1970.

Hsu, Immanuel C. Y. China's Entrance Into the Family of Nations: The Diplomatic Phase, 1858-1880. Cambridge, Mass.: Harvard University Press, 1960.

Inkeles, Alex. Social Change in Soviet Russia. Cambridge, Mass.: Harvard University Press, 1968.

The Institute of Internal and External Affairs. History of Factional Rivalry in North Korea (Pukkwe ui P'apol Tujeangsa). Seoul, 1962. U.S. Joint Publications Research Service, JPRS: 23,655, March 12, 1964.

Iriye, Akira. The Cold War in Asia: A Historical Introduction. Englewood Cliffs, N.J.: Prentice-Hall, 1974.

Kennan, George F. Memoirs: 1925-1950. Boston: Atlantic Monthly Press, 1967.

SELECTED BIBLIOGRAPHY   117

Kim, Byong-Sik. Modern Korea: The Socialist North, Revolutionary
     Perspectives in the South. New York: International Publishers,
     1970.
Kim Ch'ang-sun. Fifteen-Year History of North Korea. U.S. Joint
     Publications Research Service, JPRS: 18,925, April 26,
     1963.

Kim, Chum-Kon. The Korean War. Seoul: Kwangmyong Publish-
     ing Co., 1973.

Kim, Ilpyong J. Communist Politics in North Korea. New York:
     Praeger, 1975.

Kim Il-song. Selected Works. Vols. 1 and 2, English edition.
     Pyongyang: Foreign Languages Publishing House, 1965.

Koh, Byung Chul. The Foreign Policy of North Korea. New York:
     Praeger, 1969.

Lee, Chong-Sik. The Politics of Korean Nationalism. Berkeley:
     University of California Press, 1963.

Lee, Peter H., comp. and trans. Poems from Korea. Honolulu:
     University of Hawaii Press, 1974.

Leonhard, Wolfgang. Child of the Revolution. Chicago: Henry
     Regnery Co., 1958.

Marshal, S. L. A. The Military History of the Korean War. New
     York: Franklin Watts, 1963.

Marx, Karl, and Friedrich Engels. The Communist Manifesto,
     trans. by Samuel Moore and ed. by Joseph Katz. New York:
     Washington Square Press, 1967.

Nelson, M. Frederick. Korea and the Old Orders in East Asia.
     Baton Rouge: Louisiana State University Press, 1946.

Rudolph, Philip. North Korea's Political and Economic Structure.
     New York: Institute of Pacific Relations, 1959.

Salisbury, Harrison E. To Peking and Beyond: A Report on the New
     Asia. New York: The New York Times Book Co., 1973.

Scalapino, Robert A., ed. Korea Today. New York: Praeger, 1963.

Scalapino, Robert A., and Chong-Sik Lee. Communism in Korea.
2 vols. Berkeley: University of California Press, 1972.

Schram, Stuart R. The Political Thought of Mao Tse-tung. New
York: Praeger, 1969.

Schwartz, Benjamin I. Chinese Communism and the Rise of Mao.
Cambridge, Mass.: Harvard University Press, 1961.

Suh, Dai-Sook. The Korean Communist Movement, 1918-1948.
Princeton: Princeton University Press, 1967.

Talbott, Strobe, trans. and ed. Khrushchev Remembers. Boston:
Little, Brown, 1970.

Third Congress of the Workers' Party of Korea: Documents and
Materials. Pyongyang: Foreign Languages Publishing House,
1956.

Thornton, Richard C. China, The Struggle for Power, 1917-1972.
Bloomington: Indiana University Press, 1973.

Union Research Institute. The Case of Peng Teh-huai, 1959-1968.
Hong Kong: URI, 1968.

U.S., Congress, Senate, Committee on Foreign Relations. Background Information Relating to Southeast Asia and Vietnam.
Washington, D.C.: U.S. Government Printing Office, 1970.

U.S., Department of State. A Historical Summary of United States-Korean Relations. Washington, D.C.: U.S. Government
Printing Office, 1962.

_____. North Korea: A Case Study in the Techniques of Takeover. Department of State Publication No. 7118, Far Eastern Series, No.
103. Washington, D.C.: U.S. Government Printing Office, 1961.

U.S. Joint Publications Research Service. History of Factional
Rivalry in North Korea. JPRS, March 12, 1964.

Whiting, Allen S. China Crosses the Yalu: The Decision to Enter
the Korean War. New York: Macmillan, 1960.

Wittfogel, Karl A. Oriental Despotism: A Comparative Study of
Total Power. New Haven: Yale University Press, 1957.

SELECTED BIBLIOGRAPHY 119

Yost, Charles. <u>The Conduct and Misconduct of Foreign Affairs</u>.
 New York: Random House, 1972.

Books: Original Sources

Ch'oe Kyu-yon. <u>Chunggong ui Kundae</u> (The Chinese Communist Military). Seoul: Songumsa, 1974.

<u>Ch'olhak Sajon</u> (Dictionary of Philosophy). Pyongyang: DPRK Academy of Social Sciences Publishing House, 1970.

Han Chae-tok. <u>Kim Il-song ul Kobal Handa</u> (I Indict Kim Il-song). Seoul: Nacoe Munhwasa, 1965.

<u>Hyongmyong ui Widaehan Suryong Kim Il-song Tongji ui Chuche Sasang</u> (The Chuche Idea of the Great Leader of the Revolution Comrade Kim Il-song). Pyongyang: DPRK Academy of Social Sciences Publishing House, 1972.

<u>Kankoku-Hoku Chosen Jimmei Jiten</u> (Biographical Dictionary of South and North Korea). Tokyo, Sekai Seikei Chosakaihen (Compilations of the Research Association for the World Political Economies), 1962, 1968, and 1973.

<u>Kankoku-Hoku Chosen Yoran</u> (A Survey of South and North Korea). Sekai Seikei Chosakaihen (Compilations of the Research Association for the World Political Economies). Tokyo, 1974.

Kim Il-song. <u>Kim Il-song Chojak Sonjip</u> (Selected Writings of Kim Il-song). 5 vols. Pyongyang: Korean Workers' Party Publishing House, 1968.

_____. <u>Kim Il-song Sonjip</u> (Collected Works of Kim Il-song). Pyongyang: Korean Workers' Party Publishing House, 1953.

<u>Kim Il-song Tongji ui Nojak Saekin</u> (Index to the Works of Kim Il-song). Pyongyang: The DPRK Academy of Social Sciences Publishing House, 1970.

<u>Kuk Naeoe Chungyo Ilgi</u> (Chronology of Significant Foreign and Domestic Events, August 1945-March 1949). Pyongyang: Minju Choson Publishing House, 1949.

O Yong-chin. Hana ui Chongon (An Eyewitness Account). Pusan: Kungmin Sasang Chidowon, 1952.

Pukhan Ch'ongam (General Handbook on North Korea). Seoul: Research Institute on Communist Bloc Problems, 1968.

Pukhan Kyongje (The Economics of North Korea). Seoul: Chungang Ilbo, 1973.

Taejung Chongch'i Yongo Sajon (Dictionary of Mass Political Terminology). Pyongyang: Korean Workers' Party Publishing House, 1964.

Yi Ch'ong-won. Choson e issoso Puroryetariat'u ui Hegemoni rul Uihan T'ujaeng. Pyongyang: The DPRK Academy of Sciences, 1955.

Articles: English Sources

Abramowitz, Morton. "Moving the Glacier: The Two Koreas and the Powers." Adelphi Papers, no. 80. London: International Institute for Strategic Studies (September 1971).

Awanohara, Susumu. "North Korea: Deeper in Debt." Far Eastern Economic Review 88, no. 23 (June 6, 1975): 52.

Chang, Henry S. "Plans and Starts." Far Eastern Economic Review 55, no. 3 (January 19, 1967): 89-94.

"The Class Nature of the State." Kulloja, no. 19 (October 1963), trans. in U.S. Joint Publications Research Service. Translations of Political and Sociological Information on North Korea, no. 54, JPRS: 23,876 (March 26, 1964): pp. 1-6.

"Communique of the Eleventh Plenary Session of the Eighth Central Committee of the Communist Party of China." (Adopted August 12, 1966). Peking Review, no. 34 (August 19, 1966); p. 7.

"Comrade Kim Il-Song. The Great Leader of the Revolution, Led the Fatherland Liberation War of Our People to a Shining Victory." Korea Today, Pyongyang, no. 179 (1971): pp. 28-32.

Davies, Derek. "Traveller's Tales." Far Eastern Economic Review 89, no. 31 (August 1, 1975): 17.

SELECTED BIBLIOGRAPHY

"Embodiment of Comrade Kim Il-song's Great Idea of Chuche is the Guarantee for Victory of our Revolution." *Korea Today*, Pyongyang, no. 143 (1968): pp. 12-15.

Gayn, Mark. "The Cult of Kim." *New York Times Magazine*, October 1, 1972, pp. 16-34.

Halasz, Louis. "The Victory March." *Far Eastern Economic Review* 82, no. 47 (November 26, 1973): 22.

Herz, John H. "Korea and Germany as Divided Nations: The Systematic Impact." *Asian Survey* 15, no. 11 (November 1975): 957-70.

Hirasawa, Kazushige. "Japan's Emerging Foreign Policy." *Foreign Affairs* 54, no. 1 (October 1975): 155-72.

"Historic Lesson of the Czechoslovak Situation." Pyongyang *Times*, August 29, 1968.

"Joint Communique in Connection with the Visit of the Party and Government Delegation of the DPRK to the Rumanian Socialist Republic." Pyongyang *Times*, June 7, 1975.

"Joint Communique of the DPRK and the Soviet Socialist Republics." Pyongyang *Times*, May 19, 1969.

"Joint Communique of the People's Republic of China and the Democratic People's Republic of Korea." *Peking Review*, no. 18 (May 2, 1975).

"Joint Communique on the Visit of Nicolae Ceausesou to the DPRK." Pyongyang *Times*, June 19, 1971.

Kang, Thomas Hosuck. "The Role of Confucian Leadership and Ideology in the Political Development of Korea, 1864-1910." *Korean Affairs* 3, no. 1 (April 1973): 21-27.

Kautsky, John H. "Communism and the Comparative Development." *Slavic Review* 26 (1967): 13-17.

Kim Gum San. "In the Revolutionary Spirit of Self-Reliance." *Democratic People's Republic of Korea*, no. 137 (1967): pp. 4-7.

Kim Il-song. "The Great Idea of Lenin on the National Liberation Struggle in Colonies in the East Is Triumphing." <u>Korean Youths and Students</u>, no. 106 (1970): pp. 2-7.

---. "On Socialist Construction in the Democratic People's Republic of Korea and the Revolution in South Korea." In Kim Il-song, <u>Selected Works</u>, Vol. 2, pp. 510-60. Pyongyang: Foreign Languages Publishing House, 1965.

---. "On Some Problems Concerning Party and State Work in the Present Stage of the Socialist Revolution." In Kim Il-song, <u>Selected Works</u>, Vol. 1, pp. 288-314. Pyongyang: Foreign Languages Publishing House, 1965.

---. "On Some Problems of Our Party's Chuche Idea and the DPRK Government's Internal and External Problems." Pyongyang <u>Times</u>, September 23, 1972.

---. "On Some Problems of Our Party's Chuche Idea and the Government of the Republic's Internal and External Policies." (Answers to questions raised by the journalists of the Japanese newspaper <u>Mainichi Shinbun</u>, September 17, 1972), <u>The Agricultural Working People of Korea</u>, Pyongyang, no. 29 (1973): pp. 2-15.

---. "On the Immediate Tasks of Socialist Economic Construction." Pyongyang <u>Times</u> (Supplement), October 13, 1966.

---. "Report on the Work of the Central Committee to the Fourth Congress of the Korean Workers' Party." In Kim Il-song, <u>Selected Works</u>, Vol. 2, pp. 126-277. Pyongyang: Foreign Languages Publishing House, 1965.

---. "Speech of Kim Il-song at the Pyongyang Mass Meeting to Welcome Samdech Norodom Sihanouk." Pyongyang <u>Times</u>, August 14, 1971.

Kim, Joungwon A. "The Peak of Socialism in North Korea: The Five and Seven-Year Plans." <u>Asian Survey</u> 5, no. 5 (May 1965): 255-69.

Kim Sok-hyung, Kim Hu-il, and Son Yung-chong. "On the Grave Errors in the Descriptions on Korea of the 'World History' Edited by the USSR Academy of Sciences." Pamphlet. Pyongyang: Foreign Languages Publishing House, 1963.

SELECTED BIBLIOGRAPHY

Kim, Young C. "North Korea's Reunification Policy: A Magnificent Obsession?" *Journal of Korean Affairs* 3, no. 4 (January 1974): 15-24.

Lee, Chong-Sik. "Kim Il-song of Korea." *Asian Survey* 7 (June 1967): 374-82.

_____. "The Socialist Revolution in the North Korean Countryside." *Asian Survey* 2, no. 8 (October 1962): 9-22.

_____. "Stalinism in the East." In *The Communist Revolution in Asia: Tactics, Goals, and Achievements*, edited by Robert A. Scalapino. Englewood Cliffs, N.J.: Prentice-Hall, 1965, pp. 114-39.

Lee, Chong-Sik, and O Ki-wan. "The Russian Factor in North Korea." *Asian Survey* (April 1968): pp. 270-88.

Lee Ki-taek. "North Korean Military Policy Toward South Korea." *East Asian Review* 1, no. 2 (Summer 1974): 145-67.

Lenart, Edith. "How Peace Became Desirable." *Far Eastern Economic Review* 78, no. 45 (November 4, 1972).

Lin Piao. "Long Live the Victory of the People's War." *Peking Review*, no. 36 (September 3, 1965).

Martin, Fowler. "Pyongyang: Shedding Light on Deficits." *Far Eastern Economic Review* (August 1, 1975): p. 49.

Meyer, Alfred G. "The Comparative Study of Communist Political Systems." *Slavic Review* 26 (1967): 3-12.

Monat, Pawel. "Russians in Korea: The Hidden Bosses." *Life*, June 27, 1960, pp. 76-102.

Munthe-Kass, Harold. "Kim Il Sung: Superstar." *Far Eastern Economic Review* 76, no. 23 (June 3, 1972): 26-27.

Nakamura, Koji. "Open Door for China." *Far Eastern Economic Review* (September 2, 1972).

"National Economic Development in the DPRK, 1945-1950." Pyongyang: Foreign Languages Publishing House, 1960.

"North Korea's Neutral Course." Research Department of Radio Free Europe, August 25, 1965.

Ognev, Yu. I. "Path to Reunification of Korea and Its Enemies." Problemy Dal'nego Vostoka, no. 2 (Moscow, 1972), trans. in U.S. Joint Publications Research Service, Problems of the Far East, no. 2, JPRS: 56781 (August 15, 1972), pp. 87-98.

"On Guard of Socialist Accomplishment." Kommunist Vooruzhennykh Sil, no. 20 (October 1973), trans. in U.S. Joint Publications Service, Translations on North Korea, JPRS: 60640 (November 27, 1973), pp. 1-8.

Pak Tong-un. "Communist China's Impact on North Korea." Asea Yongu (The Journal of Asiatic Studies) 9, no. 3 (Seoul, September 1966): 49-98.

Patrick, Tony. "Park Tenses for the Challenge." Far Eastern Economic Review 83, no. 1 (January 7, 1974): 36.

"Pyongyang City Meeting Held to Commemorate the Centenary of the Paris Commune." Pyongyang Times, March 27, 1971.

Rees, David. "North Korea's Growth as a Subversive Center." Conflict Studies, no. 28 (November 1972).

"The Revisionist Clique in Korea Today." Wen-Ko T'ung-Hsun (Cultural Revolution Bulletin), no. 11 (Canton, February 15, 1968).

Scalapino, Robert A., and Chong-Sik Lee. "The Origins of the Korean Communist Movement." Journal of Asian Studies 20, no. 1 (November 1960): 9-31, and 20, no. 2 (February 1961): 149-67.

Schmidt, Dana Adams. "Does U.S. Defend Park Too Strongly?" The Christian Science Monitor, July 14, 1975.

Skillend, W. E. "Korea Today." Asian Affairs (Journal of the Royal Central Asiatic Society) 62, pt. 1 (new series vol. 6): 9-22.

Tsuru, Shigeto. "Internal Industrial and Business Trends." The Annals of the American Academy of Political and Social Science 308 (November 1956): 85-94.

SELECTED BIBLIOGRAPHY

Tucker, Robert C. "Communist Revolutions, National Culture, and Divided Nations." Studies in Comparative Communism 7, no. 3 (Autumn 1974): 235-45.

_____. "Culture, Political Culture, and Communist Society." Political Science Quarterly 88, no. 2 (June 1973): 173-90.

"The Two Countries of China and Korea Are Neighbors Which Have Relations of Lips and Teeth and People's of Our Two Countries Are Brothers Bound with Kinship." Pyongyang Times, April 13, 1970.

U.S. Joint Publications Research Service. Translations on North Korea (Kim Il-song's Tour of Eastern Europe and North Africa), no. 413, JPRS 65101 (June 27, 1975).

Yamamoto, Koichi. "My Interview with Kim Il-song." Ekonomisto (Economist), November 5, 1963, trans. in Summaries of Selected Japanese Magazines (Tokyo: American Embassy, December 2, 1963), p. 14.

Yim Seong-hi. "Thoughts of the Times." Korea Times, September 15, 1972.

Articles: Original Sources

"Chajusong ul Ongho Haja" (Let Us Defend Independence). Nodong Sinmun, August 12, 1966.

Chang Ch'un-ch'iao. "Sesang e ku Ottohan P'ungp'a ga Ilonado Chung-Cho Tu Tang, Tu Nara Inmindul un Yongwonhi Tangyolhayo T'ujaeng hamyo Kongdonguro Chonjin Halgosida" (Regardless of the Storms That May Arise in this World, the Two Countries of China and Korea and the Two Peoples of the Two Countries Will Struggle United Eternally and Advance Jointly). Nodong Sinmun, September 24, 1975.

Chi Ch'ang-ik. "Widaehan Suryong Kim Il-song Tonjikkeso nun Uri Inmin ege Minjokjok Taebonyong kwa Ryungsong ui Sae Sidae rul P'yolch'yo Chusiyossta" (The Great Leader Comrade Kim Il-song Has Opened the Way for Our People to a New Era of Great National Efflorescence and Prosperity). Kulloja, no. 4 (April 1975): pp. 41-49.

"Ch'oe Yong-kon Wiwonjang kwa Ryu So-ki Chusok Kongdong Songmyong" (Joint Statement of Chairman Ch'oe Yong-kon and Chairman Liu Shao-ch'i). Nodong Sinmun, September 9, 1963.

"Chuche Sasang ul Kuhyon hago issnun Sae Honbop un Kajang Hyongmyongjok imyo Uwolhan Sahoejuui Honbop" (The New Constitution of the Republic Which Embodies the Chuche Idea is a Very Revolutionary and Superior Socialist Constitution). Nodong Sinmun, December 31, 1972.

"Ch'ullo Minjok ui Chaju T'ongil e issta" (The Way Out Lies in the Self-Reliant Unification of the Nation). Nodong Sinmun, April 11, 1963.

"Chung ch'ao kung pao ho ch'ao hsien pan tao hsing shih" (The Sino-Soviet Communique and the Situation in the Korean Peninsula). Ta Kung-pao (Hong Kong, April 29, 1975), p. 2.

"Chungguk Inmin Chiwongun ui Choson Ch'amjon 15 Chunyon" (Fifteenth Anniversary of the Entry of the Chinese People's Volunteers into the Korean War). Minju Choson, October 24, 1965.

"Chwa-u Kyong Kihoejuui muos inga?" (What is Meant by Left-Wing and Right-Wing Opportunism?) Nodong Sinmun, January 26, 1967.

Fan Peng-t'ao. "Soren, Chugoku Shinko ni Fumikiruka?" (Will the Soviet Union Invade China?), trans. in Gendai Chugoku (Contemporary China), no. 8 (Tokyo, December 1973): pp. 102-07.

Guimard, Paul. "Le Grande Leader, Kim Il-song" (The Great Leader, Kim Il-song). L'Express, April 28-May 4, 1974, p. 81.

Ho Tam. "Uri Minjok ap e Chosongtwen Hyon Nanguk ui Chajujok P'yonghwa T'ongil ul Ch'okjin Sikilte taehayo" (Concerning Breaking Through the Difficult Situation Confronting Our Nation and Spurring the Independent Peaceful Unification of the Fatherland). Nodong Sinmun, November 9, 1974.

Kim Il-song. "Choson Minjujuui Inmin Konghwaguk un Uri Inmin ui Chayu wa Tongnip ui Kich'i imyo Sahoejuui Konganjuui Konsol ui Kangryokhan Mugi ida" (The DPRK is the Banner of Freedom

SELECTED BIBLIOGRAPHY   127

and Independence of Our People and a Powerful Weapon for Socialist and Communist Construction). Nodong Sinmun, September 7, 1968.

_____. "Chosono rul Paljon sikigi uihan Myot Kaji Munje" (On Some Problems Concerning the Development of the Korean Language). In Kim Il-song Chojak Sonjip (Selected Writings of Kim Il-Song), Vol. 4, p. 9. Pyongyang: Korean Workers' Party Publishing House, 1968.

_____. "Uri Inmin un Apurodo Chegukjuui wa Yut'ae Pokkojuui rul Pandae hayo Sae Sahoe Konsol ul Uihayo Tujaeng hanun Hyongjejok Suria Inmin ui P'yon e T'unt'unhi Soissul kosida" (In the Future Too, Our People Will Stand Firm by the Fraternal Syrian People Fighting Against Imperialism and Zionism and for Building a New Society). Nodong Sinmun, October 7, 1974.

"Kin Nichi-sei Utsunomiya Kaidan Kiroku" (Record of Talks Between Kim Il-song and Utsunomiya). Yomiuri Shinbun (Tokyo, August 19, 1975).

"Marksu-Reninjuui ui Hyongmyongjok Kich'i rul Touk Nop'i Tulja" (Hold High the Revolutionary Banner of Marxism-Leninism). Nodong Sinmun, November 17, 1962.

"Miguk Yuen ui Kyolwidaero Chagi Kundae rul Manchosonuro eso Modu Chich'e opsi Ch'olgo sikyolyahamnida" (In Accordance with the UN Resolution, the U.S. Must Remove all Its Troops Immediately from South Korea). Nodong Sinmun, November 20, 1975.

"Mijegukjuui Myolmang ul Ch'okjin sikigi uihan Widaehan Chollyak" (Great Strategy to Hasten the Downfall of US Imperialism). Nodong Sinmun, November 21, 1968.

No Tae-hun. "T'urocchukkijuui" (Trotskyism). Nodong Sinmun, September 15, 1966.

O Ki-wan. "Nodong Sinmun ui Naemak" (An Inside Account of the Nodong Sinmun). Pukhan, no. 12 (North Korea, 1974), pp. 266-73.

"Occhaeso Sungbae nun Marksu-Reninjuui Sasang kwa Inyon i opsnunga?" (Why is the Cult of the Individual Alien to Marxism-Leninism?), Nodong Sinmun, April 2, 1966.

Pak To-su. "Sahoejuui Munhwa Konsol un Chugwon ul Chabun Nodong Kyegup ui Chungyo Immu" (The Important Duty of the Working Class Which Gains Supremacy is to Build a Socialist Culture). Nodongja Sinmun, December 15, 1966.

Pang Ho-sik. "Sahoejuui Chinyong Naradul kan ui Kisul Kyongjejok Hyopjo" (Technical and Economic Cooperation Between the Countries of the Socialist Camp). Pyongyang: Korean Workers' Party Publishing House, 1958, 47 pp.

"Pukkwe ui Kanch-obson Chojak T'ongbak" (North Korean Spy Ship Operations Refuted). Choson Ilbo (Seoul, February 28, 1974).

"P'uroretaria Tokjae kwa P'uroretaria Minjujuui Ungho Haja" (Let Us Uphold the Dictatorship of the Proletariat and Proletarian Democracy). Nodong Sinmun, February 4, 1971.

"Sahoejuui Chinyong ui T'ongil ul Suhohayo Kukch'e Kongsanjuui Undong ui Tangjol ul Kanghwa haja" (Let Us Safeguard the Unity of the Socialist Camp and Strengthen the Solidarity of the International Communist Movement). Nodong Sinmun, January 30, 1963.

"3 Tae Hyongmyong ul Him Isske Pollryo Sahoejuui Konsol ul Touk Takuch'ija" (Let Us Vigorously Carry Out the 3 Revolutions and Further Accelerate Socialist Construction). Nodong Sinmun, March 5, 1975.

"Ssoryon Kongsandang Che 22 Ch'a Taehoe e Ch'amka hayosston Choson Nodongdang Taepyodan Saop e Taehayo" (On the Work of the KWP Delegation to the Twenty-second Congress of the CPSU). Nodong Sinmun, November 28, 1961.

"Suryong e Taehan Ch'ungsongsong un Kongsanjuui Hyongmyong tul ui Kajang Kibonjokin P'umsong ida" (Loyalty to the Leader is a Very Fundamental Characteristic of Communist Revolutionaries). Nodong Sinmun, August 2, 1974.

Tamaki, Motoi. "Jinmin Minshushungi no Saikento" (A Reexamination of the Theory of the People's Democracy). Koreya Hyoron Tokyo, November 1971, pp. 4-19.

Wae Pyongyang Kyongje T'oronhoe ui Songgwa rul Holttuturo hanun ka?" (Why Do They Disparage the Success of the Pyongyang Economic Seminar?) Nodong Sinmun, September 7, 1964.

SELECTED BIBLIOGRAPHY

"Widae han Suryong Kim Il-song Tongjikesso Chungguk Inmin ui Widae han Suryong Mo T'aek-tong Tongji T'ansaeng Yotuntolsul Ch'ukha hayo Ch'ukjon ul Ponaeshiyotta" (The Great Leader Comrade Kim Il-song Sent a Congratulatory Message to the Great Leader of the Chinese People, Comrade Mao Tse-tung). Nodong Sinmun, December 28, 1973.

Yi Man-kap. "Hanguk Sahoe ui Kach'i Kujo" (The Value Structure of Korean Society). Sasanggye (Seoul, May 1961), pp. 62-71.

Yi Sok-yun. "Ilbon Kungukjuuija tul ui Wihom han Kyoljong" (The Dangerous Decision of the Japanese Militarists). Nodong Sinmun, October 1, 1965.

INDEX

Acheson, Dean, 36-37
adventurism, 6, 8, 11
Afghanistan, 100
agricultural collectivization, 5, 49, 50
Albania, 34, 42, 54
Algeria, 76, 101, 104
Argentina, 100
Asiatic mode of production, 21-22

Bangladesh, 100
Brezhnev, Leonid, 88, 91; Doctrine, 4, 88
Bulgaria, 34, 42, 104
Burundi, 76

Cambodia, 76, 95 (See also, Sihanouk)
Cameroon, 100
Central Africa, 76
China (See, People's Republic of China)
Chinese People's Volunteers (CPV), 26, 30, 37-39, 40, 44, 50, 61, 71 (See also, People's Republic of China)
Cho Man-sik, 28
Ch'oe Ch'ang-ik, 30, 52
Ch'oe Yong-kon, 52, 57-58, 76, 84
Chou En-lai, 54, 76, 88, 89-91, 95 (See also, People's Republic of China)
Chu Nyong-ha, 28
chuche, 24-27, 68, 69-70, 72, 87, 112
collective leadership, 61-62
Congo Brazzaville, 76
continuing revolution, 12

Cuba, 76, 81, 92; missile crisis, 55
Cultural Revolution in China, 11, 30, 74-75
Czechoslovakia, 34, 42, 55, 88, 92, 94

Dahomey, 76, 100
de Gaulle, Charles, 88
Demichev, Petr, 67
Democratic Republic of Vietnam, 68, 71, 73-74, 75, 80, 81, 82-83, 89, 96, 101, 104; relations with, 34
Denmark, 100
detente, 6, 8-9, 11-12, 20, 88, 91, 112, 113
dictatorship of the proletariat, 10, 23-24, 56-57, 60, 94 (See also, Marxism-Leninism)
dynastic past, 13

EC-121 incident, 8, 20, 83, 112
East Germany (See, German Democratic Republic)
Egypt, 40, 100
Engels, Friedrich, 26

factionalism, 28-30, 44, 110
Federal Republic of Germany (FRG), 36, 88
France, 88

German Democratic Republic (GDR), 34, 42, 56
Ghana, 76, 81
Great Leap Forward, 61, 71, 89 (See also, People's Republic of China)

INDEX

great power politics, 9, 11, 21, 69-70, 112, 113; chauvinism, 3
Gromyko, Andrei, 97
Guinea, 76

Hegel, Georg Wilhelm Friedrich, 21-22
hegemony, 88, 92, 95, 102, 111
Ho Chi-minh, 20
Ho Ka-i, 29, 42
Hungary, 5, 34, 42
Hyon Chun-hyok, 28
Hyon Chun-kuk, 89

Iceland, 100
Inchon landing, 37-38 (See also, Korean War)
independence, 25-26, 34-35, 49, 58, 61, 68-72, 74, 87
India, 40, 55, 100
Indonesia, 68, 70, 76, 77

Japan, 1, 9-11, 13, 34, 35, 60, 77, 88, 89-90, 92-93, 96-97, 99-100, 102, 111
Japanese Communist Party, 11
Johnson, Lyndon B., 67, 82-83

Kennan, George F., 35
Khrushchev, Nikita, 5, 48-49, 52-53, 54-56, 58, 59-62, 69, 78, 88-89
Kim Chong-il, 87
Kim Chong-suk, 87
Kim Chung-nin, 92
Kim Il-song, 2, 4-5, 9, 12, 13, 19-31, 33, 35, 40-44, 48, 55, 59-62, 67-71, 73-74, 77-79, 80, 81-82, 83-84, 87-88, 89-91, 92-93, 95-96, 98-99, 102-05, 110-14
Kim Kwang-hyop, 82, 91
Kim Tae-chung, 99
Kim Tu-pong, 30

Kim Yol, 30
Kim Yong-chu, 98
Kissinger, Henry, 98
Korean War, 1, 7-8, 33, 35-36, 37-38, 39, 41-42, 44, 71, 79
Korean Workers' Party, 11, 12, 35; August 1956 Plenum, 29-30; March 1958 Party Conference, 29-30; Fourth Party Congress, 51, 54, 70, 93; Fifth Party Congress, 19, 91-94; Political Committee, 27-28, 87, 92-93
Kosygin, Alexei, 66-68

Lee Hu-rak, 98, 99
Lenin, V. I., 22-23, 33
Liberia, 100
Lin Piao, 75
Lin Yun-chuan, 89
Liu Shao-ch'i, 57-59

MacArthur, General Douglas, 36, 37
Madagascar, 100
Mali, 76
Malik, Jacob, 37
Mao Tse-tung, 20, 29, 30, 37, 38, 40-41, 49, 59, 61, 73-74, 79, 82, 91
Marxism-Leninism, 12-13, 21-25, 26-27, 41, 57, 75, 78
Mauritania, 76, 104
Mauritius, 100
Mayaguez, 104
Mazurov, Kirill T., Deputy Premier, 90
Mikoyan, Anastas, 52
Mongolia, 34, 42, 97
Mu Chong, 29, 42

NATO (North Atlantic Treaty Organization), 38
Nam Il, 11
nationalism, 13

new Socialist man, 21
Nixon, Richard M., 89, 95-96, 101; Doctrine, 88
nonaligned bloc, 104
North-South Military Commission, 101
North-South talks, 98, 100
northern patrol limitation line, 100
northern territories issue, 12
Norway, 100

O Ki-sop, 28
opportunism: left, 75; right, 75-76
oriental despotism, 21-22

Pak Ch'ang-ok, 30, 52
Pak Chong-hui, 53, 79, 80, 82, 98, 99
Pak Hon-yong, 29, 42
Pak Il-u, 29
Pakistan, 100
Pak Song-ch'ol, 11, 98
Palestinian Liberation Organization (PLO), 104
Peng Teh-huai, 39, 44, 52, 75 (See also, People's Republic of China)
people's committees, 34-35
people's democracy, 34-35
People's Republic of China (PRC), 2-4, 6, 8, 10, 11-12, 30, 33, 40-43, 49-51, 54, 61, 71-76, 78, 79, 81, 83-84, 87-91
Poland, 5, 34, 42, 94
policy mechanism, 27, 34-35
proletarian internationalism, 27
Pueblo incident, 8, 20, 80-83, 112
purges, 28-30, 48, 50-51, 70

Republic of Korea (ROK), 8, 12, 36-38, 53, 67, 71, 77, 79-81, 82, 93, 99-102, 112-13

reunification (See, unification)
revisionism, 56, 58, 68-70, 72, 75, 88-90, 92-94
revolutionary line, 1
revolutionary tradition, 10
Rhee, Syngman, 79
Rumania, 34, 42, 82

Shanghai communique, 95, 96, 113
Shelepin, Aleksander, 72
Shihanouk, Norodom, 95
Sino-Soviet relations, 1-2, 5-6, 8-9, 10, 12, 21, 35-36, 37, 39, 44, 48-49, 52, 53-57, 58-61, 75-76, 87-89, 91-92, 96, 111, 113
small powers, 13, 21, 83, 87-88, 112
socialist patriotism, 13
South Korea (See, Republic of Korea)
Soviet Union (See, Union of Soviet Socialist Republics)
Stalin, Josef, 4-5, 20, 30, 33, 35, 40-42, 48, 54; de-Stalinization, 4-5
Sukarno, 76, 77
Sweden, 100
Syria, 100

Taiwan, 38, 76-77, 102
Tanaka, Kakuei, 11, 97
Tanzania, 76
Teng Hsiao-ping, 59, 103
Third World, 95, 100, 104
Tito, Marshal, 56, 58
Trotskyism, 74-75
Truman, Harry S., 38
Tsiang, T. F., 37

Uganda, 100
unification, 11, 21, 60, 79, 98-99, 111-12, 113-14
Union of Soviet Socialist Republics (USSR), 4-6, 8, 10, 20, 33-36,

INDEX

37, 39-41, 42, 43-44, 48-50, 51-56, 58-62, 66-69, 70-72, 73-74, 75-76, 78, 81, 83-84, 88-89, 91-92, 96, 101, 102, 104-05, 111, 112-13
United Arab Republic (UAR), 76
United Nations (UN), 12, 37, 38, 88, 100-01, 104-05, 113-14
United States (U.S.), 6-9, 11, 36, 60, 81-83, 88-90, 91, 95-98, 100, 101-03, 104, 111, 112-13
Upper Volta, 100

West Germany (See, Federal Republic of Germany)
World Health Organization (WHO), 100
Wu Hsin-yu, 72
Wu Hsiu-chuan, 59

Yemen, 76
Yi Sung-yop, 42
Yugoslavia, 58, 104

Zakharov, Marshal, 90

ABOUT THE AUTHOR

WAYNE S. KIYOSAKI, a graduate in Korean of the Defense Language Institute, formerly served as a commissioned officer in the U.S. Air Force and is presently with the Foreign Broadcast Information Service.

Dr. Kiyosaki holds a B.A. from the University of Hawaii, an M.A. from the University of Michigan, and a Ph.D. from George Washington University.

RELATED TITLES
Published by
Praeger Special Studies

COMMUNIST POLITICS IN NORTH KOREA
          Ilpyong J. Kim

DIMENSIONS OF CHINA'S FOREIGN RELATIONS
          edited by Chun-tu Hsueh

INTERNATIONAL POLITICS IN EAST ASIA
SINCE WORLD WAR II*
          Donald F. Lach and
          Edmund S. Wehrle

SMALL STATES AND SEGMENTED SOCIETIES:
National Political Integration in a Global Environment
          edited by Stephanie Glicksberg Neuman

QUANTITATIVE TECHNIQUES IN FOREIGN POLICY
ANALYSIS AND FORECASTING
          Michael K. O'Leary and
          William O. Coplin with the
          assistance of Howard B. Shapiro

*Also available in paperback as a PSS Student Edition